Now the trick is to get an autographed copy. On this page here. Not that it would ever happen, but just in case. Make sure its in color and not black and white!

Autograph Page

~ more secrets revealed ~

**The complete underground
Technical Marketing guide
to kicking your competitors a****

**Based on the infamously popular first edition
"The Silicon Valley Survival Handbook"™**

*Don't be afraid of what is inside of this book. It
contains magic ... you just need to read it and dig
for it. Do what I've done. Follow these steps. Follow
these guidelines. You will uncover something truly
historical, and maybe even hysterical. The next time
you see your competitor, give them the crocodile smile,
knowing that you are undertaking a secret mission*

that will obliterate them from the marketplace.

**[Note: Parental discretion advised.
Contains material that will
blow ...
your ...
mind...]**

*This has yet to be taught in schools, even at those
pricey über elite universities.*

Technical Marketing®

Marketing II

II

the

QUIET

POISON™

release

second edition

by
Craig Thomas Ellrod

Technical Marketing
~and~
Technical Marketing II

ISBN 978-0-9822570-4-3

90000

9 780982 257043

trate
uest™

Permissions

"

*There is magic in this book. dig deep
and you will find it!*

"

Contents

1

Technical Marketing

What is Technical Marketing anyway? It sure sounds really snappy. The term originated at the beginning of the explosion of the commercial Internet. Although, after reading through newspaper articles from the 1960's and 70's, and my father's journals, I can tell you that the job of marketing technical products has been around for decades. Technical Marketing bridges the gap between engineering and sales. In a sentence it can be condensed to, "the art of bringing together significant research on a product and presenting the Delta features in a dramatic way."

But over time it has morphed into something even completely more useful than you would initially think. Technical Marketing is many things, and you will understand most of them by the end of reading this book. At least read the table of contents. Tech Mktg is the art of bending someone's perception to see your point of view. Is it deception? No, deception is the art of fooling someone into giving you something for nothing. Twisting perception is the art of changing someone's point of view to see the value and give you something in exchange for your goods and services.

" *Technical Marketing bridges the gap between engineering and sales.* **"**

As the computer industry approached the turn of the millennium (the year 2000), there continued to exist a gap between engineering and sales at various high-tech companies. Engineers were highly talented at building brilliant and powerful computer systems, and sales were equally proficient at relationship management and generating revenue. System's Engineers often times filled that gap but their focus was on revenue and not marketing. There was an increasing need for marketing talent to bridge the gap between sales and engineering, to take the products engineers had built and articulate them in a meaningful way so that sales people and systems engineers could convert them into sales revenue.

More and more companies in the Silicon Valley began to hire "Technical Marketing Engineers" to bridge the gap between sales and engineering, and to increase sales revenue. Technical Marketing has become a key role in bringing products to market and a key component in competitive strategy in maximizing industry leadership and revenue.

The discovery of Technical Marketing resulted after having been in the Computer Industry for several years, starting out as a programmer, moving into customer support then technical support. Eventually, I became what was then called a Corporate System Engineer for lack of a better term. The SE to the SE's in the field. It was a critical role bridging the gap between engineering and sales. I remember getting a call in Orange County in the late 90's to be flown to the bay area for an interview for a new position. We had talked on the phone about a new type of position, one that never existed before, it was called "Technical Marketing".

The guy that interviewed me didn't fit the mold. He had long hair in a pony-tail, Vans tennis shoes, sleeve tattoos, rode a harley and lived on 44th street in Newport Beach. He had actually flown up to Silicon Valley just to interview me. Funny, because I had been living in Huntington Beach at the time and vowed, I would never leave the surf. It was at the turn of the millennium so I guess it was a time for change. We had started what became known as a new era for the technical professional, and for me. The boom of the Internet created increased demand for technical people who understood how to market technology in meaningful and dramatic ways, because market execution had to be more precise to match declining budgets.

Product Marketing Engineers and Corporate Systems Engineers became Technical Marketing Engineers. Technical Marketeer's who could work hard, learn fast, pull together a sizzling demonstration and show off a products "Delta" features in a dramatic way suddenly found themselves becoming the rock stars of their employers. Technical people now had a growing and intense new forum to exercise and build their craft. Technical Marketing was born.

Technical Marketing is about presentation of technical products in striking and dramatic ways. Technical Marketing is about competition and strategy and the methods used to win in the marketplace.

Technical Marketing is hard work, and it is a daily struggle to keep going. When I came to valley, I was healthy. When I got married later my wife informed me of some odors and smells that I had never been aware of before. I found myself making visits to the doctor for reasons I could not understand. I don't know many guys who start out in Technical Marketing, or who get suckered into technical marketing, that actually stick with it. It is a demanding career. The profession isn't noble like the other arts, the pay is low, and the hours are long. If you genuinely enjoy the work, you will stick with it, and the work will be rewarding to you and of value to others.

The rewards for me are in peeling back the layers of the onion, not knowing what is to be uncovered next, and finding the little nuggets of opportunity that can turn into big development ideas. Since I have been doing this, there has never been a dull moment, and I truly love what I do. So, can you.

Technical Marketing started in the computer industry and has turned out to be very powerful, not only for competitive marketing, but also for the advancement of technology. Technical Marketing is competitive in nature, and incorporates some competitive marketing tactics, yet takes it to another level with more focus and aggressiveness on winning, with specific tools and deliverables to get you there.

You could argue that it feeds the engine of innovation and invention and ultimately improves the quality of products. On this basis, Technical Marketing, and the practices thereof, can be used in any industry, and there are a few that I can think of where it would help.

2
Intellectual Property

The link between Technical Marketing and Intellectual Property is indissoluble. Through research and becoming intimate with your own products you find areas for improvement. By researching the market and competition, you find areas and ideas for competitive advantage and improvement. These ideas become a groundswell for future intellectual property.

Many companies today have an invention disclosure process where you submit your invention or intellectual property discovery. There are typically groups of review teams that determine if the invention disclosure needs to be submitted through the legal department as a patent application, at which time it becomes bona fide intellectual property for the organization. In order to compete successfully today, this type of process is absolutely crucial. The more efficient this process is, the better it will be for the organization acquiring the intellectual property rights. The first to file, is the first to claim.

In this era Intellectual Property is far more valuable than physical property. It is also less tangible and easier to abscond with. Nevertheless, IP, or Intellectual Property (not the Internet Protocol), is at the core of a Technical Marketeer's being.

The benefits of Intellectual Property abound. IP allows you or your organization to take high ground in the marketplace, and gives you the legal right to do so, thereby allowing you to stake your claim for long periods of time. Hence, you can reap the benefits of the revenue stream for a much longer period of time, without contention or threat of competition. Intellectual Property comes in the form of Patents, Copyrights and Trademarks and is that medium by which you or your organization can defend itself or stake a claim in the market, should a legal battle arise over ownership of a particular technology.

There are also problems identified with Intellectual Property. It is costly to develop and maintain, it can be stolen and is frequently "borrowed", it can be misdirected and miscommunicated, it can be forgotten about, it can be left undeveloped and under-resourced. Some really great ideas never get developed because of a lack of funding, or a lack of strategic viability. Someone thinks it won't benefit the organization competitively at the end of the day, and there isn't enough money to finance it.

The Technical Marketeer always documents and keeps records of their work and progress. It is common practice to carry a lab notebook around to document meetings, drawings and ideas. Be sure to keep track of Date, Time, and Names of those involved. This information is needed to fill out invention disclosure forms and documents that describe the inventions so that anyone can understand them.

When we talk about Intellectual Property, it's hard not to bring into discussion the issue of copyrights, trademarks, patents and trade secrets. If you navigate over to the https://www.uspto.gov website, you can discover a ton of resources, including tips on how to file for these legal protections on your own. I can tell you from my own experience that copyrights and trademarks are easy to do on your own. Patent's and determining trade secrets you can do on your own, but you will likely fail, because the first thing a patent examiner will do is issue an "Office Action" which will make your head spin. Try to get a patent attorney that will work for less money. This isn't rocket science and don't let attorneys take all your money, just find one that will do the "legal" BS work for you. Patent examiners, and trademark examiners, actually respond better and listen to attorney's more than basic civilians. I know that's messed up, but that's the USPTO system for you.

Copyright

Copyright protects the expression of an idea, the illustrated content of the idea. It does not protect the idea itself – that is a patent. "Creative expression" may be captured in words, numbers, notes, sounds, pictures, or any other graphic or symbolic media. The subject matter of copyright is extremely broad, including literary, dramatic, musical, artistic, audiovisual, and architectural works.

There are some limits to copyright protection, unfortunately, and these are labeled under Fair Use such as criticism, comment, news reporting, teaching, scholarship, and research. Other limitations fall under what is called a "Compulsory License" where certain limited uses of copyrighted works are permitted upon payment of specified royalties and compliance with statutory conditions. It is also legal to use copyrighted materials for satire, library preservation, personal backups and for making specialized copies of works for people with physical disabilities, such as the blind or deaf.

Trademarks

Trademarks provide protection for specific words or graphics that represent the organization, in other words it's brand. A trademark can be a name, a logo or a phrase associated with an organization. It can also be a color or a sound, or some combination of these such as a jingle. Getting a trademark registered is relatively easy if you do your homework on the https://www.uspto.gov website. You can search for existing marks under the Trademark Electronic Search System – TESS. If you find that no-one or no organization has filed your mark, you can submit a registration application online quickly and easily. The ® symbol is used for marks that have been registered by the USPTO, and the TM symbol can be used by anyone who plans to file a registration or has filed a registration with the USPTO but it has yet to be approved.

Patents

Patent law protects inventions, the ideas that form inventions, processes, methods, materials and even plant life. There are different types of patents including a utility patent which is mostly used for inventions that have a useful purpose, a design patent for the actual design of the invention and a plant patent for .. well, plants.

Trade secrets

Trade secrets don't have formal protection, but exist as long as you keep them secret. Trade secrets are the same as intellectual property and they contain many of the same aspects as the legal protection. Trade secrets also have been found to include customer lists and clientele. Trade secrets exist at the time of creation, similar to copyrights. In order to maintain the Trade Secret, you must protect it from disclosure to the public. If it remains secret you are afforded legal protection against anyone that acquires it inappropriately. The difficulty with trade secrets, is that they can be discovered legitimately, even though competitive analysis and product teardowns, and there is no protection against this.

Designation	Symbol	Protects	Length of Protection
Copyright	©	*The expression of an idea*	*70 years after death*
Trademark	®, TM	*Name, Logo, Phrase*	*10 years with renewal*
Patent	*<patent ID>*	*The idea, design or plant*	*20 years*
Trade Secret	*<secret>*	*Your secret sauce*	*Perpetually (forever)*

13

3
Credibility

Credibility is key. Without credibility no-one is going to listen to you, or believe you. I have seen many enter the field of Technical Marketing because it appeared glamorous and sexy and filled their ego and bank account, yet never perform. I have seen many enter the field thinking they could sidestep the responsibilities of a sales engineer where there is accountability to sales numbers. Technical Marketing is much harder, if not as hard as working out in the field, because you are often called on to go out into the field to help sell the product.

Technical Marketeers have to know what they are talking about technically, which means you need to know your stuff. You also have to put the time in, in the lab, and in the field. You have to be book smart, rack smart and customer smart. I have watched guys who have been in technical marketing for years who still can't plug in an Ethernet cable, or figure out the difference between bridging and routing. These are basics, and you need to go much, much deeper than this. Often times, you have to know more than the CTO of your company if you want to do the job right.

Remember, Credibility is your mantra throughout your Technical Marketing career. Make sure you know what you are talking about. When it comes to the computer industry, always document your test network with detailed diagrams showing data flows, links, interfaces and IP (Internet Protocol) Addresses. Always back up your numbers with data that can be reproduced, by your customers. Credibility is of utmost importance to a Technical Marketeer. The only way to solidify your credibility is to back up your claims with evidence from testing and documentation.

Competitive Test

You must perform tests to prove and back up your facts. You can hire someone to do it for you, or you can do it yourself. Caveat emptor, as some of the traditional outsourced marketing test outfits will publish anything you tell them to, because you are paying them. I have read many test reports that lack credibility because they were "bought". A competitive test report must be believable, and you can't pull the wool over anyone's eyes. You can't use smoke and mirrors here. I've seen cases where the report lacks merit because the test methodology isn't even published in the report altogether, which brings into question the credibility of 1) the test house that produced it and 2) the vendor that paid for it. The best way to dig out the details is to test it yourself. You need test equipment to do this.

Specific to the computer industry, stopwatches don't exist in this field. The human eye, human hand and mechanical workings of a stopwatch are slower than the electronics being measured, and cannot provide meaningful and accurate performance data. There are legitimate tools available for measuring performance of products in the field of Technical Marketing.

Test equipment is expensive, so you will have to bite the bullet, and buy it, lease it, find a friend who has it or write your own software to do it. There are some traditional network testing favorites. There are many other up and coming network testing equipment vendors that do a much better job, with much better pricing options and much better user interfaces. There are some freebies on the internet, but they don't scale, don't perform well and don't keep track of results for you.

Performing a competitive test on your products as well as other products is important, because it provides you with the evidence you need to back up your claims. Remember that credibility is of utmost importance to a Technical Marketeer. The way to keep your credibility is to back up your claims with evidence from testing and documentation.

Competitive test involves two important components, the device under test (DUT) (or solution under test (SUT)) and the Testing Equipment. Different DUT's require different test networks. The following are examples of the several variations of physical test configurations that can and have been used in network competitive tests.

Competitive test is a critical component of Competitive Analysis, and is used in the Validation Test/Competitive Test phase.

Vendor	Popular for
https://www.ixiacom.com	IxLoad, IxExplorer, IxChariot for L2-L4 testing.
https://www.spirent.com	SmartBits for L2-L4 testing, Avalanche/Reflector for L4-L7 testing

TANSTAAFL

"There ain't no such thing as a free lunch". This is especially the case with test equipment. Test equipment is expensive, so you will have to bite the bullet, and buy it, lease it, find a friend who has it or write your own software to do it. There are some traditional network testing favorites listed later on. There are some freebies out there, but they just don't scale and the savvy buyers won't buy into the metrics or the test results you produce.

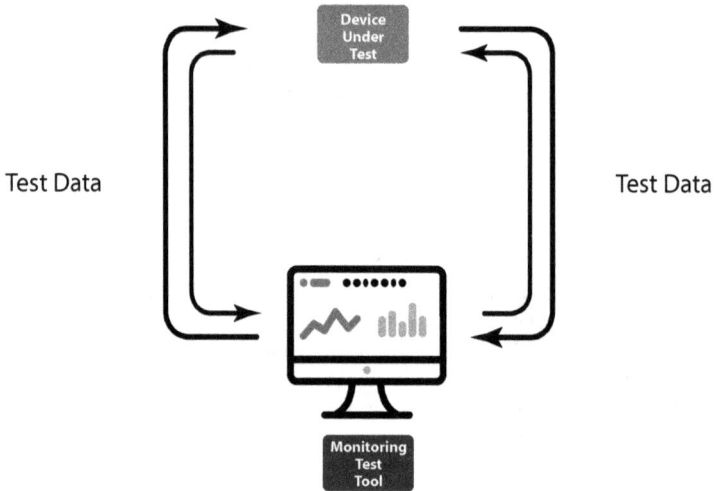

Layer 2-4 Test Network

The above illustration is an example of how you would set up a monitoring test tool and connect it to the Layer 2, Layer 3 or Layer 4 device to be tested. Data must flow bi-directionally, that is, in both directions for a valid test. The lines represent wired connections, Etherrnet or Fiber.

23

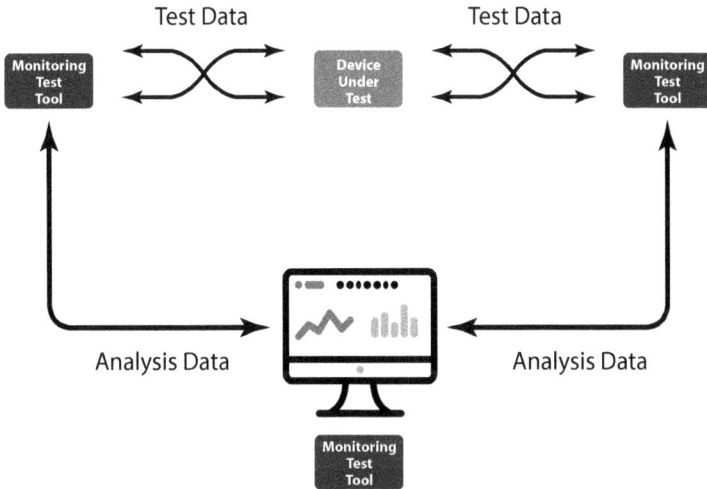

Test Data   Test Data

Monitoring Test Tool   **Device Under Test**   **Monitoring Test Tool**

Analysis Data   Analysis Data

Monitoring Test Tool

Layer 4-7 Test Network

The above illustration is an example of how you would set up a monitoring test tool and connect it to the Layer 4-7 device to be tested. Data must flow bi-directionally, that is, in both directions for a valid test. When you are testing applications, you need a client sending data and a backend server sending data, which is why there are two Monitoring Test Tools represented. The lines represent wired connections, Etherrnet or Fiber. The crossed lines represent cross-over configuraitons, when the sending interface on the monitor crosses over to the receiving interface of the DUT or application.

Cloud computing has changed our digital world recently. You almost don't have any control over the wires in your datacenter, because everything is virtual. This sort of mires testing and results a bit. If your DUT or SUT is in the cloud, how do you test it?

Excellent question. You can still do your testing, it is just that you will need to account for the infrastructure you are running on top of. For example, instead of having wires or cables connected directly to your DUT's or SUT's, you will now be sending your data over "virtual networks". That is, your network data running on top of or across the cloud provider's virtual network, which then runs on top of cable. If you're thinking latency, you are correct. Data within data, within data is bound to slow some things down and obfuscate results. The best thing you can do is run several "baseline" tests and some up with some standard performance curve that includes a margin for deviation. Then run your tests, and take that baseline into consideration. Unless the cloud provider gives you the keys to their datacenter, you really have no other option.

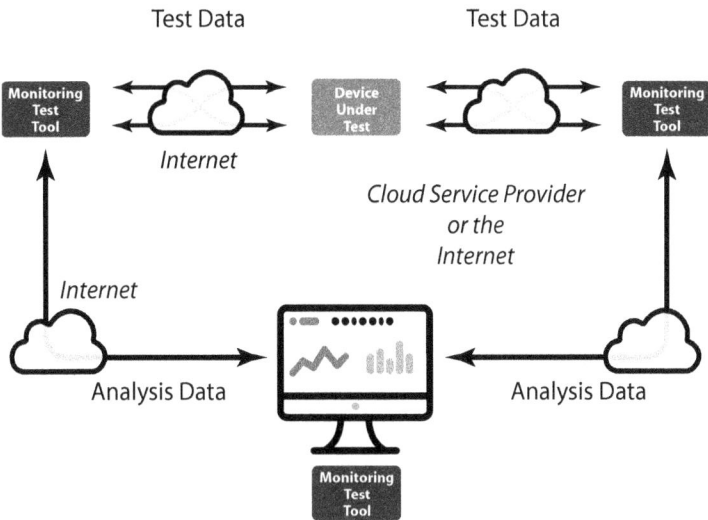

Test Data   Test Data

Monitoring
Test
Tool

Device
Under
Test

Monitoring
Test
Tool

Internet

Cloud Service Provider
or the
Internet

Internet

Analysis Data   Analysis Data

Monitoring
Test
Tool

Layer 4-7 Test Network

The above illustration is an example of how you would set up a monitoring test tool and connect it to the Layer 4-7 device to be tested - in the cloud. Data must flow bi-directionally, that is, in both directions for a valid test. The only difference is, anywhere you see the cloud icon, could represent that you are sending/receiving your test data over the Internet/Cloud infrastructure on any one of those paths. One of the more popular online tools for testing applications is called https://www.gtmetrix.com. It assigns a score and tells you which components of your application are fast or slow. There are many other alternative testing tools if you search the internet for "Web Application Performance Testing".

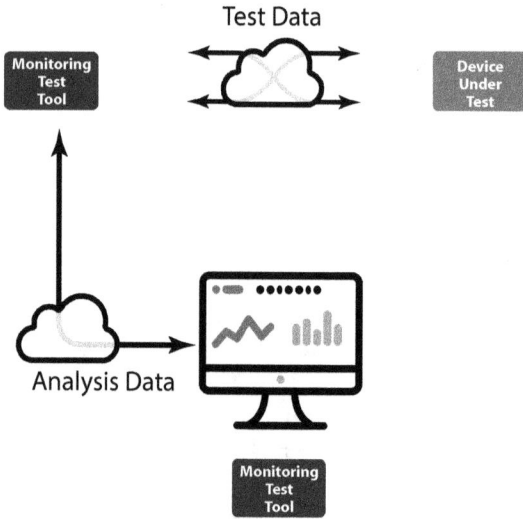

Test Data

Monitoring
Test
Tool

Device
Under
Test

Analysis Data

Monitoring
Test
Tool

Layer 4-7 Test Network

The above illustration is an example of how you would set up a monitoring test tool and connect it to the Layer 4-7 device. Sometimes it's necessary to just test the front-end interface of an application. Data must flow bi-directionally, that is, in both directions for a valid test. The lines represent wired connections, Etherrnet or Fiber. The lines can also represent connections through the Internet and/or Cloud.

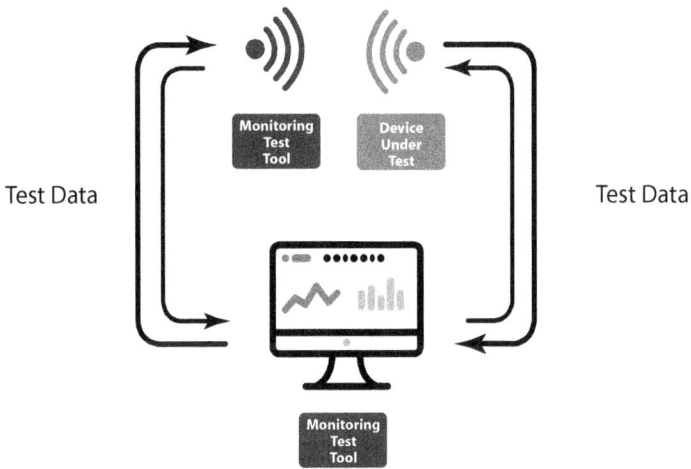

Layer 2-4 Wireless Test Network

The above illustration is an example of how you would set up a monitoring test tool and connect it to a wireless network, to test wireless network devices. More and more of our connectivity is being provided through wireless technologies, so this is very relevant. The connections to the test tools and DUT's or SUT's can be directly connected or over the Internet or Cloud. Testing wireless devices usually requires the use of a farraday cage to eliminate any other radio noise. Be sure to establish test baselines first, just in case there is interference.

5
Competitive Analysis

Competition is healthy. It is what drives the USA and the global economy's pulse. The government wants you to compete, in fact there are laws in place that protect it. I am not a lawyer so I am not going to expound the law. But I am here to tell you that it is OK to compete, and compete fiercely, as long as you do it legally. If you are not sure of the legality of your position, ask a lawyer.

You were taught in school to use SWOT analysis – strengths, weaknesses, opportunities and threats. Strengths and weaknesses are internal, opportunities and threats are external. This is cute, but not useful for Technical Marketing. It doesn't dig deep enough and doesn't explore widely enough. There is no acronym for digging deep. There is only hard, laborious work.

There are some websites that offer free competitive information. Some that offer competitive information for a fee. You can hire a team to do the competitive analysis for you, in house. Startup companies are sometimes better at competitive analysis than larger companies. Larger companies, for whatever reason, think they are invincible and take a lackadaisical approach to competitive analysis, leaving it in the hands of the sales force to gather what they can while on the run. By the way, having the field gather intelligence is a good, and important tactic for reconnaissance or information gathering on your competition. Partner's and reseller's will often give sales people anything to win business, including information on the competition. I'm not saying this is ethical, I'm just saying it happens.

Once all of the competitive information is compiled, it needs to be disseminated. The means to do this is up to the creative imagination. Some methods involve weekly updates to the field to keep them abreast of the latest competitive information and the location of the repository. Presentations, documents, spreadsheets, graphs and the like are common mediums. The biggest challenge facing competitive analysis is getting the results into the minds of the people that need it. At one company where I worked, we held regular competitive update conference calls and sent out regular messages with competitive briefs and the repository location, and people still called and e-mailed from the field asking for the latest information on "xyz company", when I had given them the information yesterday. Some of the more popular tools coming of age are Wiki's, Blogs and Partner websites, where the information is posted regularly, HTML formatted e-mails are sent out, and links in the e-mail take the reader back to the Wiki's, Blogs or Partner sites containing the latest competitive information.

Competitive Analysis is a lengthy process that can be divided into different phases.

- Research
- Validation
- Analysis
- Presentation

Research

Start with what is publicly available. The internet is your friend and you can gather so much information from it using the search engines and websites of various targets that you are researching.

Tradeshows are designed to generate leads for field sales, but have increasingly become a forum for snoops and lurkers doing reconnaissance on the latest information companies are leaking to the market. There are a lot of imposters at tradeshows sent in to draw out information that would otherwise not be available to the mainstream public. It's an interesting game when someone says they are an independent consultant.

By law public companies have to present financial statements every quarter and at the end of the year. This may or may not help you with the competitive analysis, but can give key insights into the direction a competitor may or may not take based on revenue streams.

Develop your contacts within the industry and go to lunch. Ask questions while you are there. Friends know what is going on with key projects better than any other source. Release dates, hiccups, bugs, roadblocks, key discoveries, important partnerships and mergers all play a part in competitive analysis. It's the little things that you need to pay attention to that can make or break a technology. If there is a key weakness that you discover in a conversation, or a competitive delta that hasn't been exploited, these boondoggles can be well worth the time.

Industry press does the same thing, only they are given key data from companies because they have special privileges, usually because they are going to write a press article and give some type of marketing exposure in exchange. Search these articles for stuff you might have missed, they are juicy.

Although daunting, but also a good source of information, are the various existing patents and trademarks databases online.

Pull all of this information together, take notes and store it in the Public Information File on your computer.

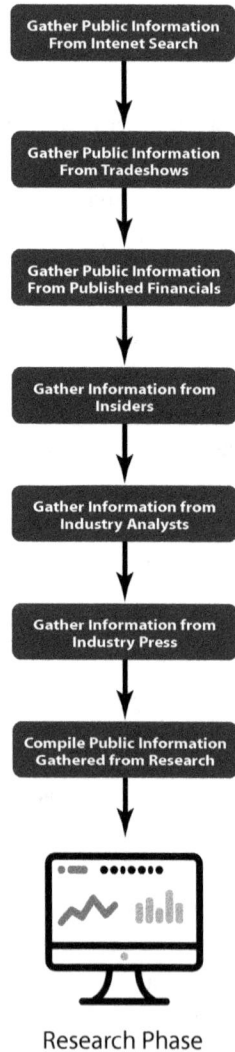

Gather Public Information From Intenet Search

Gather Public Information From Tradeshows

Gather Public Information From Published Financials

Gather Information from Insiders

Gather Information from Industry Analysts

Gather Information from Industry Press

Compile Public Information Gathered from Research

Research Phase

Validation

Whether you are performing a competitive test or validating your own product against your research, you must perform hands-on lab work. You must be technically competent and go technically deep. There is no way to cheat.

In the same way that you prepare an outline before writing a paper or book, you prepare a lab layout and network diagram before plugging in the equipment. Otherwise, you will end up with a mess. It will enable you to troubleshoot your way around once you have a network diagram.

With regards to the computer industry, the network diagram should include classic elements such as the "Device Under Test" - DUT (or "Solution Under Test" - SUT), and the "Testing Tool". Other elements commonly included in the network diagram are the IP addressing scheme (Internet Protocol), interfaces, speeds, feeds, vlans, trunks, clients, servers, traffic flows, and media types. Most media in use today is Ethernet at varying speeds. A network diagram should include two parts, the physical network layout, and the logical network layout. The physical network layout shows all of the physical connections, interfaces, cables, ports, patch panels, etc. The logical network layout shows all of the higher level connections, such as IP addressing, vlans, trunks, traffic flows, etc.

A clear statement of what is to be tested and the goals of the test should be outlined in the test methodology and test plan, so that someone else can pick up where you left off in case you get hit by a bus. In my case, I often get distracted, and have to refer to my notes.

Building out the physical or virtual network takes tried and true know-how. Either that or a desire and strong will to succeed combined with some smarts. Finding the right cables, switches, and other hardware is the easy part. Plugging that stack of equipment in and configuring it along with the DUT or SUT, Test Tools, switches, routers, racks, power supplies and getting the whole thing up and running in record time - is what takes talent. If you can pull this off in a few hours, that which takes the average person a week to do, you might have what it takes.

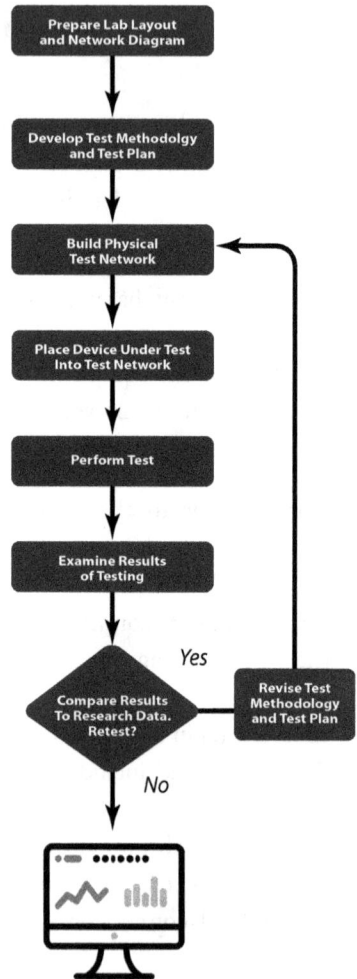

```
┌─────────────────────────┐
│ Prepare Lab Layout      │
│ and Network Diagram     │
└─────────────────────────┘
            │
            ▼
┌─────────────────────────┐
│ Develop Test Methodolgy │
│ and Test Plan           │
└─────────────────────────┘
            │
            ▼
┌─────────────────────────┐
│ Build Physical          │◄──────┐
│ Test Network            │       │
└─────────────────────────┘       │
            │                      │
            ▼                      │
┌─────────────────────────┐       │
│ Place Device Under Test │       │
│ Into Test Network       │       │
└─────────────────────────┘       │
            │                      │
            ▼                      │
┌─────────────────────────┐       │
│ Perform Test            │       │
└─────────────────────────┘       │
            │                      │
            ▼                      │
┌─────────────────────────┐       │
│ Examine Results         │       │
│ of Testing              │       │
└─────────────────────────┘       │
            │                      │
            ▼            Yes       │
        ◇─────────◇  ┌──────────────────┐
       ╱ Compare    ╲ │ Revise Test      │
      ╱ Results To   ╲│ Methodology      │
      ╲ Research Data╱ │ and Test Plan    │
       ╲ Retest?    ╱  └──────────────────┘
        ◇─────────◇
            │ No
            ▼
```

Validation Test Phase

35

Once everything is staged, the DUT (or SUT) can be faithfully placed in-line for test. But, before you do that, I highly recommend you run a test without the DUT just to get a baseline reading. Depending on if you are running "routing" vs. "bridging", this could add extra time and flavor to your test methodology.

Perform your tests, and keep track of them using spreadsheets. Save every test in a separate worksheet or spreadsheet. Every detail counts. Many test tools save results in .csv or spreadsheet format already. Remember, no stopwatches!

After the test run, or several test runs, it is time to examine the data. It is better to have more data, than less, because you might notice a competitive delta that didn't exist before. So pull all of it together and comb through it.

Look for deltas that didn't exist before. Look for high and low variances and things that don't look right or don't add up. If numbers seem to be too askew, you will have to review with a trusted colleague. I always review my results with the engineer that built the product, because they have a gut feel one way or another.

Compare results to research data. If results don't look dramatic enough to "tell a story", then you quite possibly will need to revise the test methodology and test plan (back to the drawing board), and re-test. The point is to dig-up dramatic results; however, honest and verifiable.

Note:

Some companies keep their test methodologies, test plans and test results a secret. I think this diminishes credibility. If you have done a good job, and you are the best, publish your test methodology, test plans and test results so that your customers can validate your results. It brings credibility to your organization and your product and will leave your competition in the dust as they try to catch up.

Delivery

The hardest part of Technical Marketing is delivering. You can spend all day in research absorbing information, and this can be fun. You can spend all day in the lab and never get anything done. The key is to develop a plan, sometimes written out in a *"Statement Of Work"*, which outlines what the problem definition is, what it is you need to accomplish in the lab, and what the outputs and deliverables are going to be at the end of the project. In this SOW should be a timeline of estimated workflows, so you can double check your progress and stay on track. Because, just like in show business, you are only as good as your last deliverable. And if you aren't delivering, …

Industry Analysts

Lets face it, they aren't going to be going away anytime soon, so learn how to use them to your benefit.

Sample Competitive Performance Spreadsheet

L2-4

	Your Organization Your Product Δ
Maximum Concurrent TCP Connections	1,400,000 conns
Maximum TCP Connections/Sec	25,000 cps
Maximum Throughput	1 Gbps
TCP Multiplexing Ratio	10:1

SSL

Maximum Concurrent SSL Connections	100,000 conns
Maximum SSL Throughput	1 Gbps
Maximum SSL Transaction Rate - No Session Re-Use	10,000 tps

L7 HTTP

HTTP Transactions/sec	45,000 tps

L7 HTTPS

HTTPS Transactions/sec	15,000 tps

HTTP Latency

HTTP 1.1 Latency	< 1 ms (TT1B) < 10 ms (per Web Page)

HTTPS Latency

HTTPS Latency	< 10 ms (TT1B) < 1 s (per Web Page)

[1] Some architectures don't match and cannot be validated or tested

[2] Some solutions are so flawed they cannot produce adequate results they are considered "*unproven*"

39

Competitor 1 Product x	Competitor 2 Product y	Competitor 3 Product z
800,000 conns	*700,000 conns*	*600,000 conns*
15,000 cps	*14,000 cps*	*13,000 cps*
900 Mbps	*800 Mbps*	*300 Mbps*
7:1	*5:1*	*not available [1]*
100,000 conns	*50,000 conns*	*40,000 conns*
500 Mbps	*150 Mbps*	*100 Mbps*
5,000 tps	*2,500 tps*	*1,000 tps*
30,000 tps	*25,000 tps*	*20,000*
10,000 tps	*5,000 tps*	*unproven [2]*
< 1 ms (TT1B)	*< 1 ms (TT1B)*	*< 1 ms (TT1B)*
< 50 ms (Web Page)	*< 50 ms (Web Page)*	*< 1 s (Web Page)*
< 10 ms (TT1B)	*< 10 ms (TT1B)*	*unproven [2]*
< 2 s (Web Page	*< 3 s (Web Page)*	

Analysis

You have all of your research. You've done your hands-on validation test. Now comes the fun part, competitive analysis. Here is where you supplant myth with reality, claimed with proven, not only for your own product(s), but for your competitors as well. Lay it out on the table and see where you stand. This is a good time and place for some quiet reflection in the war room. From this point the light of reality shines on the current standing of your products and future endeavors that you wish to unfold. What can be revealing at times, is that many organizations don't take the time to dig deep and accurately find out where they stand competitively.

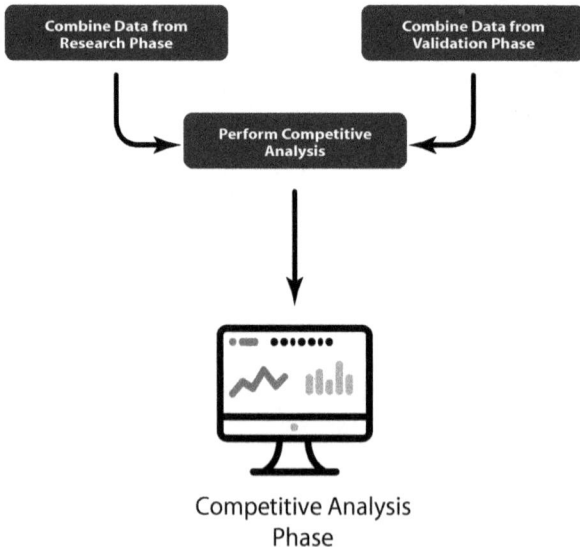

Competitive Analysis
Phase

FUD

Technical Marketeers never throw FUD. Fear, Uncertainty and Doubt are for the less noble and less adept. Everything we write and talk about has to be backed up by facts. This is your job as a Technical Marketeer, to bring credence and credibility to the technical marketing data at hand. Whether someone else has done the fact checking or testing, or you spend hours verifying the facts yourself in a lab, no FUD. Hence, your bullet is sure to pierce when it hits the target.

Claimed

Theoretical metrics based on engineering specifications. These are not always fact until proven.

Proven

Real world testing results. Metrics obtained through real world testing.

Presentation

The results of the analysis can be presented in many forms. Credibility is key, the presentation of data cannot contain any FUD or invalid data, or the field will lose trust and credibility - hence they will lose. FUD and invalid data is a weakness. Make sure your data sizzles, but make sure it is accurate.

As mentioned before, Technical Marketing involves presenting your data in "Dramatic" ways. This means not only knowing the technical aspects of the product, but knowing how to present it. There are many exciting mediums to make use of today. The simplest of which most people use on a daily basis - Microsoft Office. A competitive brief, technical document or white paper can be typed up and printed to Adobe PDF format. Granted, it gets messy when sophisticated graphics are required, but it gets the job done.

Powerpoint is good for presentations. There are many programs for the delivery of video based content and demonstrations - the crux of a Technical Marketing presentation. Technical Marketing is all about giving demonstrations in a dramatic way, which is why screen recorders such as Camtasia and Screenflick so popular. You can build a dramatic demonstration offline, and let it run indefinitely on a Blog or Tradeshow floor. With Virtual Tradeshows becoming more popular, Virtual Demonstrations will be a common venue for Technical Marketeers.

When it comes to making presentations dramatic and professional, there is no substitute for the Adobe tools, and the common format for document distribution is the Portable Document Format (PDF). All Adobe and Microsoft products output to PDF. Most all computer systems can read PDF.

Some of your material is good for public consumption, while some is even more important to the internal sales team. Nothing is more important than the competitive playbook.

Much like you see in the hands of an NFL coach on the field during a game, the playbook lists all of your products, offensive plays, defensive plays and counter attacks to the competition. Knowing your competition is important, but knowing that your competition knows you and your plays is more important. You need to know how to counter attack their attacks, defenses and trump them before you get to the playing field. A highly researched, tight, focused playbook is crucial to field sales. Most playbooks only contain the top 3-4 competitors, leaving the others for the lengthy competitive briefs and competitive presentations.

Just as valuable are regular updates in the form of competitive briefs, or announcements to the field. They should be short, one to two pages that highlight the competitive landscape and weaknesses of the competitor.

Competitive Analysis often finds it's way into intellectual property and strategic business development. It is also useful in competitive presentations, RFI's, RFQ's, RFP's, responses to analyst reports, press releases, white papers, training material, sales presentations, industry reports, Market Requirement Documents (MRD), Product Requirement Documents (PRD), product roadmaps, partner enablement, and of course performance analysis documents.

Data from competitive analysis can also find it's way into data sheets, frequently asked questions (FAQ) documents, hot sheets, battlecards, fast fact sheets and customer presentations. The practical usefulness of the competitive research serves many needs, but the two that keep recurring are fighting the everyday battles in field sales against the competition, and long term strategic planning. If you don't have the facts, you won't be successful at either.

Competitive analysis data has been finding its way into online knowledge bases and reports for free or fee. The most compelling and useful competitive analysis documents that make use of this data are the competitive briefs and the competitive playbook. Playbooks should be short and concise, because on gameday, your troops will have already done their month long studying of the competition, they just need factual bullet points as reminders for execution. If it is too long, people won't read it. Getting to the customer first is the best strategy, because you can play your offense, and "*lay your traps*" for the competition, leaving them tongue tied and unprepared when they do arrive.

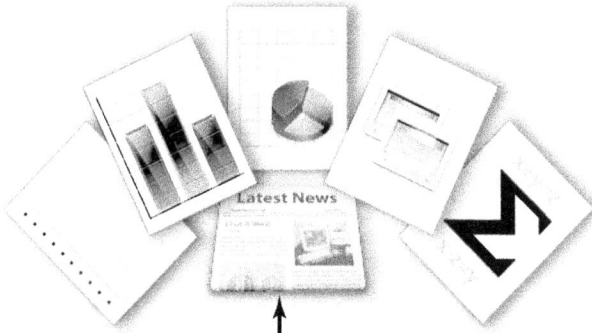

Presentation of
Competitive Data

The Technical Marketing Wheel of Death and Domination

The Competitive Analysis process we just walked through is be known as the Technical Marketing Wheel of Death and Domination™. This is where you discover the magic that you wield. It is your data, truth and facts compared to your competitors data, truth and facts. You will discover things that will enlighten your point of view. More importantly, you will discover things about your competitors, that even they don't have a clue about. This is where this is off the hook fun. You can even rebrand the wheel to your liking to make it even more fun. For example, "<insert your funky name here> Wheel of Death", or "<your company/project name> Wheel of Domination". This is how you use the Technical Marketing Wheel of Death and Domination. In the middle of that Wheel is the Pool of Knowledge that you have gained from the process, along with the Tools, Tactics and Procedures for wielding that knowledge. If you are a startup company you obviously can't afford to buy a bunch of lab gear in addition to your competitors

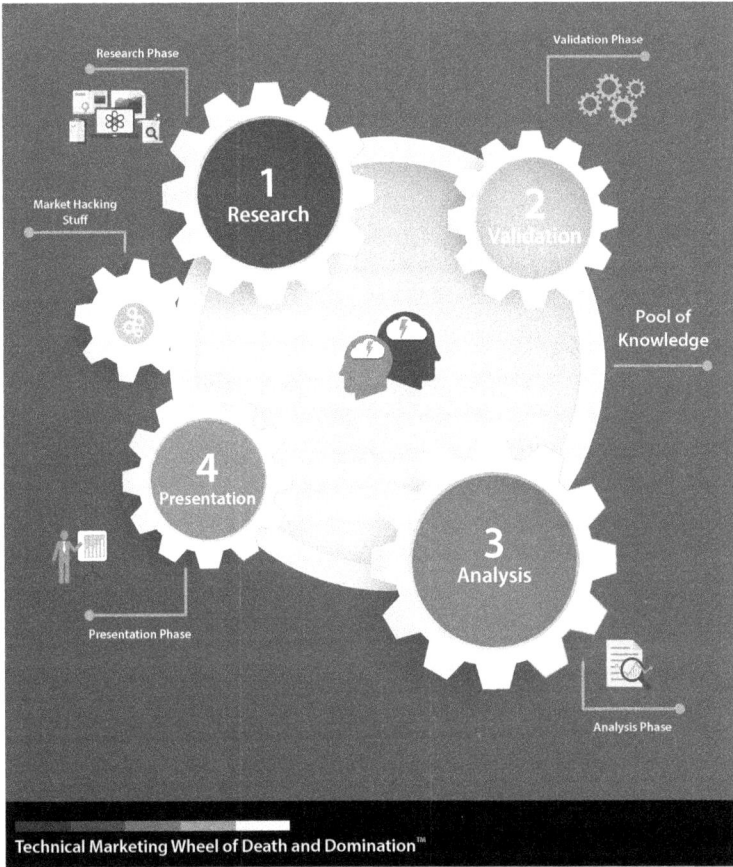

Technical Marketing Wheel of Death and Domination™

products. You may have to just focus on what you can get your hands on, even if it's just Research, Analysis and Presentation.

Sample Statement Of Work

Project Overview

A brief and overview of the project

Project Objective

The Objective is to:
- Show the value of x and y solution working together
- Asses Scalability of x and y solutions
- Test and prove performance of x and y solutions

Project Owners

Stakeholders and contributors who are accountable for the deliverables at the end of the project.
- Name, e-mail, phone.

Project Environment

Details for the lab environment:
- Physical environment (IP Addresses, etc)
- Logical environment
- Diagrams
- Detailed list of products and versions

Project Deliverables

The output at the end of the project.
- Interoperability report, Scalability report, Performance report
- Competitive Brief, Competitive Playbook
- Video tip, Demonstration script, White Paper

Project Timeline

Estimate of project workflows and workplans. Use a spreadsheet.

Estimates, Expenses and Change

- List Responsible parties for costs and expenses.
- Provide a change management process, to CYA.

Engagement Agreement

- Stakeholders and Contributors Sign or Agree on the SOW.
- An agreement is in place to keep the project goals on track.

49

Sample White Paper

Introduction

A brief Introduction

Problem Statement

Describe the problem you are solving
- List all of the problems you are solving.
- Customers have pain, so address it here.
- ...

Previous Options

Discuss how it used to be
- The risks and downsides to staying the course and not changing.

Proposed Solution

Solutions have to provide Benefits, not features, so write about them. Talk about how you solve the problem.
- Benefit 1
- Benefit 2
- Benefit 3

Summary

Summarize
- Restate the problem
- State how you solved the problem

Conclusions

Be brief, be concise, be a thought leader.

Sample Invention Disclosure

Title of Invention

Title is usually descriptive of the invention.

Inventors

Name, Address, Citizenship, Department, Contact Information.

Background of the Invention

Describe in general terms the purposes and object of the invention.
- Include drawings, flowcharts, sketches, note pads, papers, meeting minutes, meeting notes, diagrams, etc., which help with understanding and evaluating the invention.
- List Prior Art or Closest known technology.

Description of the Invention

Describe the Invention in detail so that another competent person in the field would be able to understand it.
- Describe each step in the process and what it accomplishes.
- Provide test results, List any referenced patents or publications.

Advantages of Invention

- How Invention differs from Prior Art.
- Describe the problem that the Invention solves.
- State what is "New" in the Invention.
- List the advantages of the Invention over the current state of the art.

Alternatives

- Describe other forms of the invention.
- Other means of accomplishing the same thing.

Record of Invention

Date first conceived?, Physical record? Whom did you disclose to? Disclosure date?, Evidence of disclosure?

Public Disclosure

- List papers, abstracts, internet postings, presentations, sales, offers to sell, planned readiness, etc.
- Public disclosure sometimes results in loss of patent rights.

Signature

- Name, Signature of Inventor, Date

Sample Competitive Brief

Executive Summary

A brief and concise description of the findings.
- The three top bullet points that readers should be aware of
- ...
- ...

Discussion Points

A list of all key findings from competitive analysis in paragraph or bullet form.
- List all of the weaknesses
- Some readers need to know all of the dirt
- You may need to refer back to this during a heated, drawn out competitive battle.
- ...

Where does the competitor mislead the customer

List the juggernauts
- They always leave something out, that could cause the customer some grief
- ...

Performance

Every customer deserves to know the true performance
- Educate the customer on what the competitor hasn't told them
- Cite your sources, even if you did the testing
- ...

Pricing

Its always about money
- Compare the price of the solutions in column format side-by-side
- ...

Conclusions

Be brief, be concise, be fierce.

Sample Competitive Playbook

Offense

Propose to customer	Your Company, Your Product Delivers
Key Benefit • Concise description Why? • Explain the compelling Impact to customers business	• Delta Feature Δ^1 • Delta Feature Δ^2 • Delta Feature Δ^3 • ... • *etc*
...	...

Defense

Customer will ask you
Key Benefit • The competition has ...
...

53

Competitor 1 Response, Your Counter Response	Competitor 2 Response, Your Counter Response	Competitor 3 Response, Your Counter Response
Competitor: • Our Product does $\mathcal{X}^1$ • Our Product does $\mathcal{X}^2$ Your Response: • Reveal facts that disprove the claim • Remind customer of weakness of competitor • Refocus customer on your Delta features • *etc* ...	Competitor: • Our Product does Ψ^1 • Our Product does Ψ^2 Your Response: • Reveal facts that disprove the claim • Remind customer of weakness of competitor • Refocus customer on your Delta features • *etc* ...	Competitor: • Our Product does $\mathcal{Z}^1$ • Our Product does $\mathcal{Z}^2$ Your Response: • Reveal facts that disprove the claim • Remind customer of weakness of competitor • Refocus customer on your Delta features • *etc* ...

Competitor 1 Claim, Your Counter Response	Competitor 2 Claim, Your Counter Response	Competitor 3 Claim, Your Counter Response
Competitor: • Our Product does $\mathcal{X}^1$ • Our Product does $\mathcal{X}^2$ Your Response: • Your product does Δ^1, Δ^2, Δ^3 • Call out your Delta Features • Remind customer of weaknesses of competitor • • *etc* ...	Competitor: • Our Product does Ψ^1 • Our Product does Ψ^2 Your Response: • Reveal facts that disprove the claim • Refocus customer on your Delta features • Remind customer of weaknesses of competitor • *etc* ...	Competitor: • Our Product does $\mathcal{Z}^1$ • Our Product does $\mathcal{Z}^2$ Your Response: • Reveal facts that disprove the claim • Refocus customer on your Delta features • Remind customer of weaknesses of competitor • *etc* ...

54

Sample Organization Profile

Organization/Company

Name

Address

Contact

Public or Private

Founded

Headquartered

Number of Employees   *(geographic split, departmental split)*

Annual Revenues   *(last three years. profitable/unprofitable)*

Expected Revenue Growth   *(for next twelve months)*

Rounds of Venture Capital   *(include all rounds of VC raised)*

Debt

Cash

Profit Ratio on Product(s)   *(ex: 85% profit margin)*

Mission Statement

Product

Current Product(s)

Version(s)

Release Date(s)

Software, Hardware, Both

Feature Set

Architecture

Integration with Standards

Availability and Performance

55

Sample Organization Profile

Product...cont'd

Target Market

Vertical, Horizontal, Both

Market Driver   *(key market opportunity)*

Value Proposition   *(why the customer buys)*

Planned Features   *(next set of advanced features)*

Missing Features   *(according to your customers)*

Customers

Number of Customers   *(by geography)*

Number of Units Sold

Reference Customers   *(list the top five)*

Key Delta Features   *(ones that solve customers problems)*

Typical Customers Profile   *Large Enterprise (over 1000 users)*
                                       Small to Medium Business (under 1000 users)
                                       Service Providers

Typical Customer Sale

Customer Satisfaction Rating

Strategy

Sales Strategy   *(direct, channel, partners, combination)*

Key Partners

Key Competitors

Pricing of Product

Annual Licensing Cost

Annual Support & Maint Cost

6 Product Teardowns

What does a product teardown have to do with Technical Marketing? In the world of Technical Marketing, a product teardown represents the process of breaking down a product to its individual components, and then finding a way to design and construct a new and improved product. It also involves analyzing the strengths and weaknesses of the products produced by the competition. Product teardowns can really help your strategy when it comes to the competitive side of Technical Marketing.

In this chapter, we will clearly define a product teardown, the benefits of committing to the process, and some of the best practices used by cutting edge companies when it comes to performing product teardowns. We will also examine what to avoid when conducting a product teardown, as well as list a few examples that have turned several products into niche leading performers.

What is a Product Teardown?

Also referred to simply as a teardown by product specialists, a product teardown represents the process of completely taking apart a product for a number of reasons. You might perform a product teardown to identify each component, as well as understand the functionality of each component. Some product teardowns involve analyzing secret components, which are components that you would otherwise think don't exist.

However, the results of most product teardowns for products like consumer electronics are usually shared via lists and photographs. The sharing of a product teardown allows you to analyze what works and what does not work for individual products. This allows you to use the product teardown information to compare the effectiveness of competitor products compared to yours. As we will see, a product teardown represents an integral part of a competitive analysis. It is also a powerful method that allows you to use component information, without having to conduct a product teardown. Shared product teardowns happen frequently in the battery and semiconductor industries.

Let's examine the semiconductor example. Professionals within the technical community can discover the latest components used to design and manufacture semiconductors for products such as the Apple iPhone and Wii video game console. Product teardowns help techies understand how a product works, as well as introduce cutting edge features. Product teardowns also provide insight into the cost of materials utilized to design and manufacture products. Knowing the cost of materials allows companies to develop more accurate production budgets. Because many manufacturers are not allowed to disclose a list of components used to make products because of non-disclosure agreements, product teardowns create the information companies need to evaluate the effectiveness of products. Teardowns also play a vital role in court hearings, especially litigation that involves product defect claims.

Product teardowns are frequently conducted to help companies improve the manufacturing process. The process starts with sketches that are relevant to a certain product's designed, followed by the input of additional ideas to enhance product performance. A teardown also allows a company to note component details, as well as perform additional research that helps increase the speed of the production process. Some companies conduct product teardowns as a type of exercise that builds teamwork among the professionals working on the project.

Benefits of Performing a Product Teardown

A product teardown is conducted methodically and hence, the methods used to analyze the components of a product typically lead to accurate conclusions for researchers. It involves looking at the entire assembly of a product that includes the following metrics:

- Materials
- Type of packaging
- Method of assembly

Each of the three metrics gives researchers insight into the ways to enhance the design of a product, as well as discovering if there is a strategy that will streamline the manufacturing process. One of the most important advantages of a product teardown is that it can be conducted on one of your company's products and a similar product designed and manufactured by a rival company.

Commercial product teardowns are performed on products currently available for sale. Technical teardowns occur in research labs under the coordination of a private and/or public sector organization. In either case, a teardown provides information that helps companies save money on the manufacturing process. Moreover, extended research into the components of a product improve the quality of the product. The most effective product teardowns are partnerships between a retailer and the manufacturer that supplies a particular product for the retailer. Producing innovations such as new assembly techniques and lower recycling costs are two of the benefits recently achieved by product teardown collaborations.

Because of a product teardown, many manufacturers learn about assembly steps that can be automated or even eliminated in the quest to save money on the manufacturing process. Manufacturers can also discover what components are not needed to develop a high quality product, which also lowers the amount of money spent on the manufacturing process. Here are four more benefits related to the assembly process:

- Lowers inventory costs
- Automation eliminates the need for costly manual labor
- Removes one or more unnecessary assembly steps
- Replaces one or more inefficient assembly steps
- Shortens the amount of time it takes to get a product from the design stage on to a retailer's shelf

Answers to Critical Questions

If you and your team are planning a product teardown, you probably have several questions to ask that will help you learn more about one or more of your products, as well as a product or two designed and manufactured by a competitor. Since there are apparently dozens of questions to ask, we want to narrow the list to five answers to critical questions that pertain to a product teardown.

How Much Planning Will I Need to Do?

The answer to this question is a huge "depends." No two product teardowns are alike because each organization performing product a teardown has different reasons and different products to analyze. A product manager for a computer monitor company will have different reasons for performing a product teardown than the reasons held by a product manager that wants to analyze the components of a complex marinara sauce.

Will I See Reduced Costs Because of Design Changes?

A vital part of a product teardown is to find ways to reduce the cost of designing and constructing a product. You should perform product teardowns for both new and currently available products to discover ways to reduce the costs of production. Conducting a product teardown should let you know the most effective way to cut costs, whether that involves eliminating a component or using less expensive, yet just as effective materials for component production.

How Does a Product Teardown Reduce Manufacturing Costs?

A successful product teardown should offer at least one recommendation on how to reduce the number of manufacturing cycle times. It also should alert you to more efficient ways to manufacture a product, which could mean eliminating one or more production steps or decreasing the number of team members that are responsible for assembling the product.

For software products, this would relate to labor hours to build something. Tearing down a software product might enlighten you to other techniques or packages that reduce the amount of work that needs to be done.

How Do I use a Teardown for Competitive Marketing?

A consideration for competitive marketing, is to notice that during the teardown process, you have the ability to understand where your competition is weak, and where you can gain strength. For example, using a low-end cheap semiconductor may result is lower performance, so it might be worth it to you to invest in higher-end components to gain a competitive edge. In software, you can increase competitive leverage by incorporating more usability, finding source code that already exists, and even discovering techniques that you didn't know existed yet.

How are My Competitors Doing in This Product Category?

Another important part of a product teardown involves comparing how competitors are performing in the same product category. A successful product teardown demonstrates how your products stack up in terms of price and quality. You can review product teardowns for identical products by referencing online resources uploaded by competitors that perform teardowns of the same products. They are typically found on company websites to give both consumers and distributors insight into how a product performs in the same market.

Preparing for a Product Teardown

Have you heard the official motto of the Boy Scouts? It is "Be Prepared," and that motto is appropriate to use for the professionals charged with conducting product teardowns.

The first order of business is to establish the criteria used for performing a product teardown. You have to know what you want to look for before you begin looking for it. The first step involves everyone in the company that is responsible for either designing or manufacturing the product in question. Then, you select the product that best covers every one of the criteria established in step one. The manufacturer must be able to present drawings and schematics of the product, as well as photographs if the product in different phases of production. A process schematic displays every step in the design, manufacturing, and packaging process. You should have access to a components list and installation instructions as well.

Now comes the fun part. A project manager selects members of both the design and manufacturing teams to request feedback on the current design and manufacturing process. The engineering team adds its two cents by suggesting changes to the product's design and production. A purchasing agent then provides data that gives everyone involved in the product teardown information about the costs that come with each component. Requesting the input of manufacturing line professionals offers insight into the entire assembly process.

Let's take a look at how a semiconductor manufacturer might prepare for a product teardown. The project manager will recruit members of the technical and engineering staff that have vast in-depth knowledge about the components that comprise each semiconductor product. Members of the manufacturing team will offer advice on how to improve performance of a semiconductor, with a focus on streamlining the production process. Since most semiconductors are a bit pricey, input from the purchasing manager is vital to determine which components are the most susceptible to volatile raw materials prices.

Proper preparation for a product teardown is mostly predicated on keeping open lines of communication. The project manager must clearly indicate what components the design and production teams feel require the most scrutiny. Communication can come in the form of personal interactions, as well as electronic modes of communication like email, phone calls, and text messaging. Of course, a team of highly trained professionals are recruited to disassemble the product in question, as well as put it back together in its modified version.

How to do a Product Teardown

Product teardowns typically unfold within the facility of the primary manufacturer. The location allows team members to collaborate on the disassembly and assembly of products in real time. However, advanced technology that includes artificial intelligence is poised to replace in person product teardowns in real time over thousands of miles. The transition to computer lab based product teardowns is expected to come full circle within the next decade. One of the advantages of the current in person product teardown process is every team member is easily able to learn about the number of components that are required to manufacture a certain product. Real time participation by team members also reveals the complexity of the teardown process, as well as the amount of time it takes to perform each of the manufacturing steps.

Disassembly involves team members taking apart a product component by component. The disassembly of a product allows team members to understand the interconnections between components, which facilitates a consensus for design enhancements and addresses any product quality concerns. Ultimately, project team members want to know the cost implications of making qualitative changes to a product. Team members discover issues with the manufacturing process and identify steps in the process that can be removed to improve manufacturing efficiency. Every team members documents the entire product teardown process in detail by taking notes and shooting photographs. At the end of the disassembly part of the teardown project, the team comes up with ideas to improve the design of the product.

The Teardown Report

After the disassembly phase of the product teardown project, the time arrives to produce a meticulously put together teardown report. The teardown report presents the technologies used to manufacture a product, as well as list every component installed to complete the product. Clients usually dictate other facets of a product teardown report, but the technologies used and component list should be a part of every product teardown report. The primary goal is to discover the total production cost of the materials used as part of the design and manufacturing process, while maintaining high quality, usability and customer satisfaction.

What Happens after a Product Teardown?

After the teardown comes the critical point when project team members create a priority list for product design and manufacturing changes. The recommendations can be on the feasibility of integrating specific types of production technologies. The recommendations can also be to build an entirely new product, or even introduce different software techniques and designs. If a certain technology has been proven to work, then the idea moves up to a high priority status. Technologies that exist, but require tinkering, become medium priority technological changes. Low priority changes refer to technologies currently under development. It usually takes a few weeks for the completion of a product teardown, although for high tech products, the process can take much longer. If your teardown process requires "product testing" then the process could take even longer.

Best Practices for Conducting a Product Teardown

Now that we have learned about the general aspects of a product teardown, let's examine a few more specific practices that help improve the end result of the project.

Set Up Properly

We already have mention the importance of preparation, as it often dictates the outcome of a product teardown project. As part of the preparation for a teardown, setting up involves assigning different professions within the team different tasks to perform and monitor. For example, engineers can handle the technology element of a teardown, while quality control team members ensure the delivery of a high quality product. This requires the setting of clear objectives for each sub-team. You might need hardware engineers for semiconductors or hardware products. You might need software engineers for software based products.

Feasible Work Schedule

Another element of the preparation for a product teardown is to establish a workable project schedule. The project leader should confer with each department assisting with a teardown to understand what other time constraints each team faces. In a perfect world, every member of the product teardown team should clear his or her work schedule to devote the entire workload on a teardown. Otherwise, you can expect project delays. In addition, create a teardown work schedule and stick with it as much as possible. A good place to post the project schedule and assigned tasks is in the war room.

Involve Suppliers

Material suppliers can play an important role in generating design and cost saving ideas. In fact, most suppliers have a better idea about imminent price fluctuations that are caused by changes in supply and demand. The supplier experience with manufacturers also includes the development of benchmark components that set the high quality standard for each industry.

Suppliers can sometimes provide you with key competitive insights to your competition.

Credibility is Key

You want the outcome of the product teardown report to carry a significant amount of credibility. This is accomplished by ensuring every member of the teardown team possesses the professional credentials to work on the project. Moreover, make sure every type of methodology used to complete a teardown is transparent. Make sure you are being truthful, honest and realistic in your findings.

Carefully Defined Product Component Criteria

Categorize each product component in subgroups that make sense in terms of functionality. Then prioritize which component subgroups to help the team focus on the most important components of a product.

Finally, follow the 80/20 quantification rule. Spend 80 percent of the project time developing a rough assessment. Then, devote the remaining 20 percent of the product teardown refining the teardown report's conclusions.

What to Avoid When Performing a Product Teardown

For every product teardown project, team members must not only implement the best practices, but also avoid the pitfalls that can severely derail the project. Let's review some of the worst practices of a product teardown.

Narrow Focus and/or Expertise

Making a product teardown too narrow in scope wastes the intellectual talent delivered by other team members. For example, if a product teardown is all about achieving the goals of the engineers on the team, the other team members will feel left out. Thus, the contributions given by the left out team members will be marginal at best. Make sure to ask for the expertise of every department that participates in a product takedown. In an unusual twist, this type of project requires a broader approach to focus.

Comparing the Wrong Products

Product teardowns are the ultimate failure when you do not compare apples to apples. Technical Marketing requires a competitive analysis between two products. For tearing down each product, the products must have identical specifications. Compare two products that share identical features, price points, and value propositions within the same commercial niche.

Inexperienced Supplier or Reseller

We have emphasized the importance of involving suppliers and resellers in product breakdowns, especially when it comes to alerting team members to pending material price changes. However, by working with inexperienced suppliers, you run the risk of performing an incomplete product teardown. By inexperienced, we are not referring to experience in the industry in which the supplier works. We are referring to experience participating in product teardowns, even mock ones that act as the "Spring Training" for product teardown teams.

Concept Phase Takes Too Long

The best way to avoid inaction during a teardown is to keep the concept development phase short and to the point. You have to make decisions quickly that have staying power. Prolonging the concept phase is a recipe for turning a product teardown into a backroom brawl because of the loss of patience with the process.

Lack of Structure

Yes, you want a product teardown to allow for flexibility in what gets examined and quantified. Nonetheless, any product teardown you participate in better have a well-thought out agenda that ensures the entire team gets the most out of the process.

Examples of a Product Teardown

As mentioned earlier in this chapter, the semiconductor industry is one of the greatest beneficiaries of product teardowns. In fact, all high tech products benefit from conducting product teardowns, as technology continues to advance at light speed. Moreover, prices for the materials used to manufacture high tech components fluctuate wildly, as the law of supply and demand has more relevance in the high tech sector than it has in any other industry outside of food production.

Look at Apple as a prime example of the power generated by performing a product teardown. For numerous years, Apple has constantly refined the approach to designing and constructing its world renowned line of iPhones. How has the high tech giant managed to remain ahead of the competition? Part of the answer is by conducting extensive product teardowns of its wildly popular line of iPhones. By disassembling a current rendition of an iPhone, Apple can learn how to build the new and improved version of the Smartphone for tomorrow. Everyone from engineers to online marketers to semiconductor suppliers offer input during Apple iPhone product teardowns.

Product teardowns are not limited to the high tech industry. Automakers also rely on product teardowns to race towards the top of the sales list. Teardowns performed by automakers run the gamut from a comprehensive examination of a current model to the inner workings of a safety feature, such as lane assist or blind spot monitoring. Once again, an auto manufacturer like Chevrolet involves every department in the product teardown process. As with Apple, digital marketers are playing an increasingly important role in setting the direction for product design and development. In fact, the way Apple approaches a market, is they think of what the customer wants or should have to being with, then they build in everything behind it, people, process and technology to build that product. This is what gives Apple such an edge on usability. Much of the impact of competitive marketing comes in the form of marketing implemented after the best possible user experience is determined.

In general, the producers of complicated machines and equipment can benefit from product teardowns because the projects reveal cost, quality and usability issues. From large appliances to massive agricultural equipment, the product teardown process often leads to rapid changes that dramatically alter the function of a machine or a piece of equipment. John Deere has helped farmers and landscapers cut costs by conducting frequent and exhaustive product teardowns.

Product Teardown in the Classroom

There is no better place to learn about the workings of a product teardown than by simulating the process in the classroom. Not just any classroom, but in the classroom located at one of the most prestigious universities in the United States.

For more than 10 years, some of the students attending the Massachusetts Institute of Technology (MIT) have taken courses that discuss the product teardown process. Over the past five years, students have been conducting simulated and real product teardowns.

David Wallace, who is a professor of mechanical engineering at MIT says, "We talk about needing to learn about your competitive products to understand best practice and how things are done because your goal is to be better than the competition. And now we actually go through the teardown process in the classroom."

In the simulated teardown exercises, each team has 45 minutes to take apart a product. Then, the teams utilize a pegboard to develop a display that permits observers to understand how the product works. The pegboard also displays the product components. According to professor Wallace, practice product teardowns allow students to organize resources, as well as learn how to collaborate in a team focused environment. "The class is a group of 15 people, and it's broken down so different people do different tasks," said Wallace. "You really can figure out a huge amount of product information in an hour." This is huge for a company that wants to be highly competitive and highly customer focused.

For each product, professors ask students to list something like the following information:

- Product name
- Product purpose
- Target customer
- Estimate volume of production
- The cost of the product at retail
- Location of manufacturer
- Estimated cost of labor
- Cost of the most and least expensive component

Students then have to provide the material, the method of construction, and the number of times a component was used in the design and manufacturing of the product. Students have the resources for materials and component labels available for use in the classroom.

Successful product teardowns at MIT disassemble products into the most minute components, as well as optimize the space on a pegboard for educating observers about the product. Students are also judged about how well they used photographs and whether they placed the correct labels on the right components.

Do You Have What It Takes?

Do you have what it takes to perform a successful product teardown? One of the keys is to avoid the temptation of obsessing with how the business down the block designs and constructs a similar product. The issues that surround your product will not be solved by mirroring the competition. Nor will you rise to market domination by offering a "mee too" product, that is just like the competitions.

Competitive marketing requires at least a fundamental understanding about how each of the businesses competing with you in the same niche are designing and producing an identical product.

The primary goal of a product teardown is disassembling a product and then learning how to improve its performance, quality and usability, while reducing the cost of production. By analyzing the competition, you learn about best practices, but you do not want to construct a product that looks and operates just like your closest competitor. Yes, it is a fine balancing act, but you can perform the balancing act by following all of the tips for performing a product teardown mentioned in this chapter.

7

Delta Features

Delta features take you to high ground. They fall out of the competitive analysis. Delta features combined with competitive analysis form the basis for Technical Marketing. Find features that your competitors don't have, and use them to your competitive advantage.

Some companies just outright buy smaller companies to acquire Delta features to gain high ground in the marketplace, also known as growth through acquisition. Getting bought is an exit strategy that many smaller companies seek, once they have fought well in the marketplace.

Delta features are those that competitors don't have, and you have a confirmed need for them from your customers. They can involve everything from physical design, usability, ease-of-use, and practical applicability to performance.

A good example of this is when the traditional router company in the valley offered it's operating system on a single monolithic software image, which when problems occurred would crash and take down the entire router along with all of the connections on that router.

Switch competitors developed the first modular operating system, with components linking into the switching and routing operating system that if a problem occurred, the independent modular systems would remain running while the problematic module would be troubleshot. This was a huge Delta and allowed competitors in the Silicon Valley to shift a significant portion of market share from the incumbent.

Marketing Warfare

Technical Marketing is War. Dig up the dirt on your opponents and exploit them to no end. Play to win every battle, and conquer the war. However, there are times when you need to recognize when you can't win, and live to fight another day.

Marketing warfare is like a full continental confrontation intertwined with a series of battles. Some short, some long. This isn't new information, and it probably won't change anytime soon, because we are all trying to win by hoarding the most money at the end of the game. btw: When is the end of the game?

You have to pick your battles, but as a Technical Marketeer your job is to help win the war by winning the battles. There are many theories and strategies to fighting these battles. And there are a lot of books to read to add to your arsenal. I try to keep my list short and simple and use that which I know works, because most of my time is spent in the trenches fighting and strategizing. Some of my favorites for inspiration over the years have been:

- The Art of War
- The Art of Peace
- Marketing Warfare
- Blue Ocean Strategy

There are only a couple of large companies in Silicon Valley that are perverse enough to use "The Art of War" against it's own employees to tear itself apart from the inside out. If you are going to use any of these tactics, don't use them on your fellow employees, use them on your competitors. Recommending The Art of War to a competitor is a good competitive tactic, because it has the potential to send them on a course for self destruction. Just be sure that you understand "The Art of Peace" and when to use both. There are some good lessons in The Art of War, however, there are better lessons in The Art of Peace.

I remember coming across the phrase in college, "*Quiet Poison*". When I think of Technical Marketing, I always think of that phrase. There are always going to be a handful of well known strategies. It is up to you to find some not so well known strategies that work for you, and keep them to yourself as "*Quiet Poison*" to help you win your battles. Remember, you are fighting your competitor.

Some of the older, well known strategies from The Art of War,

- "Gain the advantage and you win, lose the advantage and you die"
- "Complete victory is when the army does not fight"
- "Those who know when to fight and when not to fight are victorious"
- "A victorious army wins first and then seeks battle"
- "Induce opponents to come to you, and their force is empty"
- "Incite opponents to action in order to find out their patterns of movement and rest"

- "Foreknowledge must be obtained from people who know the conditions of the enemy", .. and probably the best of them
- "Keep your friends close, keep your enemies closer"

One of the best lessons that can be learned from "Marketing Warfare" is that strategy should be developed from the ground up, not the top down.

In playing offense and defense, you will get attacked and will need to counterattack, that is given. Your competitors are anticipating counterattacking you. It used to be that smaller companies attacked and larger companies defended. This is no longer the case. Neither size nor market share no longer dictate whether to play offense or defense. These tactics can be used in offense or defense to achieve the overall strategy.

Developing Strategies

When you and your competitor have both read all of the strategies together and are up on the game, it's time for you to discover a new strategy, or look for another unsuspecting one. Because they are going to be using the tactic that you just read about, against you. When you find a method or tactic that works against the competition, you keep it close.

The Best Marketing Tactic

The best marketing program that is in use today, and it continues to kill the big gorillas, is 'its free'. Give your software away, proliferate the market with it and undermine your competition. Make it abundant, useful, and credible. If the market accepts it and it is good, it will multiply. Now you can use your imagination on how to draw revenue from this model and companies are doing it successfully. Large companies cannot compete because they need big margin's to support their infrastructure.

The War Room

Set up a war room. If you are serious about competitive marketing and want to do it right, you will have a war room, with access limited to only those on the team. Think it's silly? This is how WWII was fought and won. Get whiteboards installed on all the walls from ceiling to floor. Map out your plans, put up the timelines. Use large 3'x4' post-it boards that can be pasted to the wall, torn down and saved in case they need to be re-used in a patent application.

G2

"Competitive Intelligence" - The term G2 has been around for many years. G2 is the name of the intelligence branch of the military. In modern tech marketing speak, Getting the "G2" on the competition refers to getting the inside information on a competitor that could help your team win the battle, or even the war. How? If you know what your competition has secretly planned to come to market with to strategically "leap-frog" your team, you can "go-beyond" them even further or secretly take high ground without them suspecting it. Thus, G2 has evolved from the wartime battlefield to the modern day marketing battlefield, and is commonly used to refer to *"Competitive Intelligence"*.

There is a book I referenced called Blue Ocean Strategy. It's a good read if you want to buy the book. It is better to just recognize the model. Blue Ocean Strategy refers to a new ocean, that has never been discovered every before. In other words, a new market where there are no competitors ... yet. In terms of gaining high ground, these little nuggets of opporunity don't come along often, but when they do ... seize them.

Strategy	Tactic
First Call	Get to the customer first, others have to follow in the wake of your tail.
Frontal Attack	Find the weakness in the competitors strength and attack it.
Flank	A move into uncontested ground, you've found a feature or new market opportunity and make a move for it.
Fence	Find a market small enough to defend.
Block	You missed an opportunity, but recover by copying the competitors move.
Neutralize	Make your competitor irrelevant.
Take High Ground	Take high ground and you win.
Attack Yourself	Improve your position by obsoleting existing ones, re-invent yourself and your products.
Value not Price	Focus on Value, not Price.
C-Level	Establish relationships with top level executives.
Open Source	Free. Give it away in the form of open source.
The Elephant in the Room	No-body can see it except you
Quiet Poison™	The one that everyone else missed.
Retreat	Know when to leave the battlefield.

Effect

Getting to the customer ~or~ market first allows you to lay your traps and establish your "*mantra*" as industry standard. Competitors struggle to "*match*" the bar you have set.

Attacking their weaknesses won't take them down, attacking their strengths will. All competitors have weaknesses in their strong points. Attacking their weaknesses doesn't hurt either.

Provides an element of surprise, catching the competition off-gaurd, leaving them tongue-tied and spinning precious cycles to catch up to you. Through relentless pursuit, a new market can achieve critical mass.

Reduces the size of the battleground, so the larger competitors can't attack you.

Allows you to maintain your position and keep competitor from getting established. When you are the leader, it is easier to do this.

Removes credibility of the value of the competitor and/or their product.

High Ground is being #1 in mind-share and market-share. It is easier to defend high ground, so you can focus energy on other strategies.

It is harder to hit a moving target, competitors struggle to keep up.

Don't get into a price battle, you will lose - "*money*".

Establish yourself as an industry thought leader and trusted advisor, and it will be easier to get meetings and get them to sign your purchase orders.

It will spread virally throughout the marketplace as it's usefulness becomes apparent. Some startup companies have actually spawned from open source projects - giving them a Blue Ocean.

It's the Elephant in the room and why isn't anyone doing this?

A competitor killer, you keep to yourself and within the team.

Save your resources to live and fight another day.

9
Creating Value

Your job as a technical marketeer is to find value, exploit it and market it endlessly. Your job is to find the key "Deltas", or value points that your product has over the competition, and exploit those "Deltas" and market them.

Caveat; I've seen many companies slapped together like art projects overnight, run through some investor funding and never really grab acceptance in the marketplace. The product or service you sell must be tangible and it must be fundamentally good. One of the startups I worked for in the valley had a product that was fundamentally good, in fact excellent compared to the competition, and it just needed to be exploited and marketed. It was pure joy pulling the competitive "Deltas" out of that product, marketing them, and slamming the competition. We really put the heat on the competition.

Part of the art of being a technical marketeer, is finding what exists that is already valuable and exploit it. If no value exists, it is your job to articulate the value to those who can take action to create it. If it is your job to create value, then you are in the wrong position and need to move into product management. By the way, the move from technical marketing to product management is a very natural step and happens quite often in the business. Once an individual knows the details of a company's product inside and out, they are then in a tremendous position to leverage that into creating the next generation of knockout products. Not all companies realize this effect, yet the payoff is big. All too often companies hire the old tried and true product manager that is better at managing schedules, spreadsheets, vendors and meetings, than at creating vision and inspiring brilliance among the product teams.

Venues for Validating Value

- Customer Advisory Councils
- Roadmap Meetings
- Partner Certification Programs
- Hosted Customer Events
- Tradeshows

Part of the function of competitive analysis is to show you where your product stands relative to the competition. As you gather data, and validate through research and testing, you will uncover weaknesses in your own product(s). This information is not to be let out to the public, although your competitors will find out about it if they haven't already, and will use it against you.

When you discover a weakness, it becomes an opportunity for improvement. Not only an opportunity to improve, but to leap frog the competition. When a you find that you have a weakness through your analysis, you prepare the same competitive brief that you would prepare to the field, however, this brief is only shown to product managers and top level executives so that they can take appropriate action. Mark the brief confidential and not for distribution.

Value is in the eye of the customer. You cannot create value if the customer does not see it your way. So, while creating value, it is of utmost importance to validate your Delta's with a real need, that is, customers who will buy it. The best way to do this is to get in front of the customer, present the ideas and get feedback. Feedback can be obtained directly from field sales, system engineering and customer support who know the direct pulse of the customer base. The delicate balance is gathering feedback without revealing too much forward thinking intellectual property such that competitors might get hold of it. There is otherwise no substitute for face-to-face meetings with customers.

10
Maximizing Spin

My good friend from Montreal who I used to travel with frequently, would always say to me, "It is in the *speen*"! What he meant was, it is in the "Spin". The key to flavoring your sell. You have heard of spin doctors and spin masters, or spin meisters. Well, prepare to become one. I am at a disadvantage having only learned one language throughout my career; however, I know it well. Take the time to know every nuance of your language as you will need to speak, write, type, scribe, record, compose, create, letter, phrase and voice your thoughts, actions and words in the most prolific and passionate manner possible.

Remember the interview question right out of college, "sell me this pencil"? I'm not so sure what kind of answer the interviewer would expect. The answer I think they were looking for was not so much a description of the pencil, but a demonstration that you had tapped into your deep creative inner being, dug deep down in your heart, felt the passion within, pulled up every sizzling, enticing word from the depths of zeal, and exhaled a sweet sentence in an iambic pentametric song in which, when finished, that person had been mesmerized into following you home. I know that's a little over the top, but you get the picture.

Maximizing spin is about passion of syntax, words, delivery and intonation. It is equally opposed to melancholy. It is about selling the sizzle. But what gives your language spin, is the passion that comes from within. When you have the ability to match a prolific writing and speaking style with your passion, you can become a spin master.

The language of business is English, so learn it well. I have worked with people from Montreal, Brazil, Africa, Croatia, Russia, Singapore, Japan, Australia, the Middle East and India, and

Technical Evangelists

Evangelism has it's roots in religion and the promoting thereof. Technical Marketeers are Evangelists, being those who enthusiastically promote technology in an attempt to build adoption in a market space.

they all speak English. I have travelled to Germany, France, Ireland, Spain, Sweden, China, Thailand, Mexico, Canada and of course England for business and the people there all speak English. Even on the Great Wall of China, they speak English.

Native languages and dialects are wonderful and interesting and make the world a wonderful place to live and visit, but when it comes time to doing business, everyone speaks English. It is important to master the English language in addition to the technical skills of racking and stacking equipment and making it come together as a working solution.

Arguably one of the best marketing documents ever written in the history of the world has it's roots in Latin, as does the English language - The Bible. Becoming a Technical Evangelist and evangelizing your word is the great aim of technical marketeers.

A dramatic writing style comes with practice, there is no way to cheat. There are tools to help. I use a dictionary, a thesaurus and the web constantly for looking up definitions to inspire my

97

thoughts when writing. Plagiarism is not allowed, your pen and tongue must be unique. Spell check and thesaurus are built into the Adobe and Microsoft products.

Mastering the spoken word as well as the written word is part of the delivery of spin. Writing and creating art with passion is only half of it. Speaking is the other half. I still have a fear of audiences, but not as much as I used too. I used to get tongue tied, sweat profusely and not make any sense. You have to get past that point, so that you know what you are talking about and speak with enthusiasm and power, so that people at least think you know what you are talking about.

Practice, practice, practice. Even the most polished executives continue to practice. I remember getting started with Toastmasters. I've taken public speaking classes and I recommend you do as well. In fact, one of the best recommendations given me was that I enroll in acting and improvisation classes, which I did. Not only was this fun, but it brought out a funny side of me, and allowed me to be comfortable in my own skin on a stage, or video camera in front of an audience.

11

The New Marketing

I'm an old-school Technical Marketing Engineer, and one day I read a job posting for "Technical Marketing" which alluded to someone who knew how to use Adobe Photoshop and could design Web Pages. I laughed at the description while a lady friend of mine did not. I took that moment to heart, and realized that technical marketing is always turning a corner. The skill sets were at different ends of the spectrum. I went back to school to learn the Adobe products. Lets face it, Microsoft word and publisher don't hold a candle to the Adobe tools. They don't anchor and render images and text properly. Adobe doesn't support Microsoft, and Microsoft doesn't support Adobe, and probably never will. Your career depends upon the quality of your work. Once I learned the Adobe products, I kept looking out across my horizon to keep it from becoming a bore-izon. Technical Marketeers must always be on the lookout for creative ways to evolve our art and craft.

Technical Marketeers have to be positive leaders for change in their field, because many times you are being looked at to take that role. As my father always used to say "Lead, follow or get out of the way", being a retired industry executive.

Web $\mathcal{X}$.0 is all about fresh, fast and exciting content. This is a medium we can take advantage of with greater ease and efficiency than ever before, because you don't have to learn HTML, although it helps. The opportunities and venues for technical marketing are turning a corner. There are new places to market ourselves, our products and services. They are coming in the form of community websites, social websites, viral marketing, acceptance based marketing and value based marketing which carries with it a high credibility rating factor.

By now everyone already knows HTML and CSS. The cost of hosting is so inexpensive, you can host many sites and domains on one service provider for pennies on the US Dollar. This is leverage.

Many startup companies and many investment funds are now outsourcing what was thought to be a talent that was not outsource-able ~ Marketing. I think you will see a lot more outsourced technical marketing, outsourced product marketing and outsourced product management to professional firms that can hire talented individuals that can handle 4 to 5 projects per person, at a lower cost to the company paying for the outsourcing. The talented individual can actually make a higher income than if they were hired full-time for one company. I know that I could personally handle 4 to 5 technical marketing projects for 4 to 5 companies, which is a far better use of my time, and a better use of the marketing expense dollars for those companies, not to mention the reduction in employee expense on the books.

New Tools Being Used

Hack the Market™	Combines Technical Marketing, Competitive Analysis with Growth Hacking and Pirate Metrics methodologies.
Pirate Metrics AARRR	Dave McClures pirate metrics for startups.
Growth Hacking	A new term coming out of Silicon Valley, focusing on rapid customer acquisition and revenue growth.
Wikis	Dynamic websites that power community websites, capable of accepting fresh, richly formatted content. Also used for Knowledge Management systems.
Blogs	Short for Web Log, is a dynamic web site, with commentary, events, descriptions, graphics, videos in a continuous chronological order. Blogs contain videos, photos, music, podcasts... everything 'new' related to marketing. Blogs are the fastest way to get your word evangelized and indexed into search engines.
RSS Feeds	Really Simple Syndication. Web Feed formats used to publish blogs a related works around the web quickly as they happen. Used for blogs, news headlines, audio, video.
Forums	Internet forums, or message boards are online discussion sites that evolved from the old bulletin board systems. They are now web applications where you can spread your word with rich content, and get it indexed into search engines. Forums are usually part of community websites. Most large companies now have community websites.
Widgets	A small chunk of code that is embedded in a web page or on a computer desktop. Now these are being used for marketing or as tiny little portals to draw people to main websites, especially for revenue generation.
Gadgets	Cool and dynamic content for websites and desktops, similar to widgets, and serve the same marketing function.

103

New Tools Being Used

Voice Overs	Put some voice on top of the video tip, and it doesn't have to be your original, there are tools to obfuscate. Make yourself sound like a sportscaster.
Podcasts	Audio or video distributed over the Internet by RSS Feed to portable media players and personal computers.
Webcasts	Audio or video distributed over the Internet using streaming media technology. Much like a radio broadcast, a Webcast can be distributed live or recorded.
Virtual Tradeshows	Replicate the activity and impact of the real thing, using the Internet, driving down costs, saving time for attendees, and zeroing in on targets for prospectors.
SEO (rank juice)	Search Engine Optimization - The art of getting listed at the top of page when someone uses a search engine. The key to getting to the customer first, the best strategy to winning.
Social Networks	Networks with values, visions, ideas, dependent upon the people that tie them together, is now a concept taking shape as websites and forums as a venue for marketeers.
Community Websites	Community websites are popping up all over the Internet to bring together groups of similar beliefs, resources, preferences, needs, thoughts, learning for the greater good. They are turning out to be places for credibility proving and acceptance based marketing. Customers now have a forum to publicly voice approval, disapproval and help others. This is powerful for those who can harness it.
On-Demand Publishing	Choose from several, do a search online. Writing a book, producing a DVD or Video can be done on your own, quickly, inexpensively. You don't need an advertising firm to do marketing.
Video Tips	Short videos that can be embedded within websites, blogs, forums, wikis for demonstrations, evangelism, news headlines, etc.

12

Tools of the Trade

Vendor	Tool
Full Stack Testing	
IXIA	Toneladas*
Spirent	Toneladas*
...alternatives	Toneladas*
Network Monitoring	
Wireshark (Ethereal)	Wireshark
Wildpackets	OmniPeek
(Vivai) Network Instruments	Observer
TCPDump	tcpdump/libpcap
Etherape	Etherape
Solarwinds	Solarwinds
Web Application Testing, Monitoring, Debugging**	
Postman	Postman
Google	Developer Tools
Mozilla	Developer Tools
Fiddler	Fiddler
Spirent	Avalanche & Reflector
Micro Focus	Loadrunner
WAPT	Web Application Testing Tool
cURL	cURL

* a ton of stuff (Spanish)

** It is worth mentioning that many of the popular browsers, Chrome, Firefox, Safari, Edge ... now have developer tools built in to them, just search for developer tools.

Location

https://www.ixiacom.com

https://www.spirent.com

... search for ixia and spirent alternatives ...

https://www.wireshark.org

https://www.savvius.com

https://www.viavisolutions.com

https://www.tcpdump.org

https://etherape.sourceforge.io

https://www.solarwinds.com

https://www.getpostman.com/

https://developers.google.com/web/tools/

https://developer.mozilla.org/en-US/docs/Tools

https://www.telerik.com/fiddler

https://www.spirent.com

https://www.microfocus.com

https://www.loadtestingtool.com

https://curl.haxx.se/

Vendor	Tool
WAN Simulation	
Apposite Technologies	Linktropy
Packetstorm	Toneladas*
iTrinegy	Toneladas*
VoIP Testing	
IXIA	Toneladas*
Spirent	Spirent VoIP
GL Communications	Toneladas*
Wireless Testing	
IXIA	IXIA Veriwave
Spirent	Spirent Wireless & Mobile
Lightpoint	Lightpoint
Web Application Security Testing	
Trustwave	Cenzic Hailstorm
Micro Focus	WebInspect
Paros	Web Security Auditor & Proxy Tool
Web Applications with Built-in Security Vulnerabilities	
OWASP	Toneladas*
Badstore	Badstore
Database Security Testing	
Trustwave	DB Protect, AppDetective Pro

* a ton of stuff (Spanish)

Location

https://www.apposite-tech.com

https://www.packetstorm.com

https://www.itrinegy.com/

https://www.ixiacom.com

https://www.spirent.com

https://www.gl.com

https://www.ixiacom.com/products/ixveriwave

https://www.spirent.com

https://www.litepoint.com/

https://www.trustwave.com

https://www.microfocus.com

... somewhere on sourceforge ...

https://www.owasp.org

https://cyb3r-cod3r.blogspot.com/2017/04/badstore-vulnerabilities.html

https://www.trustwave.com

Vendor	Tool
Security Testing	
Trustwave	Security Testing Suite
IXIA	Toneladas*
Spirent	Toneladas*
NMAP	Network Mapper
Tenable	Nessus
Metasploit	Metasploit
HPing	HPing, HPing3
Kismet	Kismet Wireless
DSniff	DSniff
Aircrack	Aircrack NG
...more at...	
Network Tools	
Solarwinds	Subnet Calculator, TFTP Server
Subnet Calculator	Subnet Calculator
Colasoft	MAC Scanner, Ping Tool
IpSwitch	Toneladas*
FileZilla	FTP Client & Server
SmartFTP	FTP Client
Cute FTP	FTP Client
Core FTP	SFTP, FTP
WinSCP	SFTP, FTP, SCP
PuTTY	SSH & Telnet
Open SSH	SSH
Open VPN	VPN
Bitvise	Bitvise Tunnelier SSH Client
Bitvise	Bitvise WinSSHD SSH Server

* a ton of stuff (Spanish)

111

Location

https://www.trustwave.com

https://www.ixiacom.com

https://www.spirent.com

https://nmap.org

https://www.tenable.com

https://www.metasploit.com

http://www.hping.org/, https://tools.kali.org/information-gathering/hping3

https://www.kismetwireless.net, https://tools.kali.org/wireless-attacks/kismet

https://www.monkey.org/~dugsong/dsniff

https://www.aircrack-ng.org/

https://sectools.org

https://www.solarwinds.com

http://subnet-calculator.com/cidr.php

https://www.colasoft.com

https://www.ipswitch.com

https://www.filezilla-project.org

https://www.smartftp.com

https://www.globalscape.com/cuteftp

http://coreftp.com/

https://www.WinSCP.net

https://www.PuTTY.org

https://www.openssh.com

https://www.openvpn.com

http://www.bitvise.com/download-area

http://www.bitvise.com/download-area

Vendor	Tool
Wireless Monitoring	
Aircrack NG	Aircrack NG
Wireshark	Wireshark
Wildpackets	Wildpackets
Tamo Soft	WiFi Tools
Presentation Tools	
Adobe	Toneladas*
Microsoft	Word, Publisher, Powerpoint, Excel, Visio
Corel	Paint Shop Pro
Colorcode Picker	Color Picker
Color Picker	Color Picker
Techsmith	Snagit Screen Capture
Typography	
Adobe	Adobe Fonts
I Love Typography	Font Website
1001 Free Fonts	Free Fonts
Acid Fonts	Free Fonts
Fonts	Commercials Fonts
Urban Fonts	Free Dingbats
DAfont	Free Fonts
Font Squirrel	Free Fonts
Blog Software	
Wordpress	Wordpress Blog Software
Wordpress Themes	Wordpress Themes

* a ton of stuff (Spanish)

Location

https://www.aircrack-ng.org/

https://www.wireshark.org

https://www.savvius.com

https://www.tamos.com

https://www.adobe.com

https://www.microsoft.com

https://www.corel.com

https://www.colorcodepicker.com

https://color.hailpixel.com/

https://www.techsmith.com

https://fonts.adobe.com/

https://ilovetypography.com

https://1001freefonts.com

https://acidfonts.com

https://fonts.com

https://urbanfonts.com

https://www.dafont.com/

https://www.fontsquirrel.com/

https://www.wordpress.org

https://themeforest.net

Vendor	Tool
Voice & Audio Software	
Adobe	Audition
Twisted Wave	Twisted Wave
Audacity	Audacity
Magix	Sound Forge
GoldWave	GoldWave
Steinberg	Cubase
Apple	Garage Band
Apple	Logic Pro X
AVID	Pro Tools & Tons of others
Linfei Ltd	Voice Recording
Video Tools	
Adobe	Premier Pro - Video Editing
Techsmith	Camtasia Screen Recorder
Telestream	Screen Recorder
Screenflick	Screen Recorder
Applian Technologies	Video Conversion Tool
Xilisoft	Video Conversion Tool
Smart Soft	Video Conversion Tool
AVS 4 YOU	Video Conversion Tool
Animation Tools	
Animaker	Animation Tool
Animoto	Animation Tool / Video Tool

Location

https://www.adobe.com

https://twistedwave.com

https://sourceforge.net/projects/audacity/

https://www.magix.com

https://www.goldwave.com/

https://www.steinberg.net/en/home.html

https://www.apple.com/mac/garageband/

https://www.apple.com/logic-pro/

https://www.avid.com/

https://apps.apple.com/us/developer/linfei-ltd/id441500559

https://www.adobe.com

https://www.techsmith.com

https://www.telestream.net/

https://www.araelium.com/screenflick-mac-screen-recorder

https://www.applian.com

http://www.xilisoft.com/

http://www.pazera-software.com/

https://www.avs4you.com

https://www.animaker.com/

https://animoto.com/

Vendor	Tool
USB Stereo Microphones	
MXL	MXL 990 USB Stereo Condenser
Blue	Blue Yeti, Yeti Pro, Yeticaster
Shure	MV88
Recording Studio Tools	
Harlan Hogan	Porta Booth
Podcast Software	
Adobe	Audition
Audacity	Audacity
Buzzsprout	Podcast recording & hosting
Apple	Garage Band
Logic Pro	Logic Pro
Hindenburg	Journalist
Alitu	Alitu
Auphonic	Auphonic
Scribie	Audio Transcription
Ringr	Podcast
Jingles & Other Royalty Free Music & Audio Clips	
Envato Market	Royalty Free Audio
Sound Stripe	Royalty Free Audio
Premium Beat	Royalty Free Audio
Music Radio Creative	Toneladas*
Voice Overs	Voice Overs
Voices	Voice Overs
Voice Bunny	Voice Overs

* a ton of stuff (Spanish)

Location

http://www.mxlmics.eu/microphones/900-series/990-USB-stereo/

https://www.bluedesigns.com/

https://www.shure.com/en-US/products/microphones/mv88

http://harlanhogan.com/portaboothArticle.shtml

https://www.adobe.com

https://sourceforge.net/projects/audacity/

https://www.buzzsprout.com

https://www.apple.com/mac/garageband/

https://www.apple.com/logic-pro/

https://hindenburg.com/products/hindenburg-journalist

https://alitu.com/

https://auphonic.com/

https://scribie.com/

https://www.ringr.com/

https://audiojungle.net/

https://soundstripe.com/

https://www.premiumbeat.com/

https://musicradiocreative.com/

https://voiceovers.com/

https://www.voices.com/

https://voicebunny.com/

13
High Performance Teams

High performance products and market leaders come from high performance organizations. I have been successful at Technical Marketing on my own. I have also built highly successful teams. It can be done either way, however, there is more power in numbers. How do you create the environment that will encourage employees to work together successfully to achieve successful critical mass?

An essential element of getting everyone on the same page is securing an ownership of responsibility from each employee down to the lowest level of the organization - creating an on-going program to develop and maintain their ownership, their personal responsibility for producing results. Also recognizing when you've got a bench warmer vs. a star player early on will be crucial to your success. You can't have any bench warmers on your team, it must be all star players. Recognizing technical competence vs. technical incompetence early on can make or break the team.

> **It is the ownership of responsibility to achieve their own results, that unleashes initiative and provides satisfaction and achievement.**

Some would argue that developing buy-in is merely a step in effective delegation or delegating to the proper level. For delegation to be effective, however, a framework of support must be in place - a framework for reinforcing consistent practices throughout the organization that rewards people for producing outstanding results.

A business operating on a foundation of objectives which every employee is committed to achieving, provides the focus for performance. Clearly defining and obtaining employee commitment to achieving the objectives directs employees toward meeting or exceeding objectives. When employees are performing together on that level, it generates high morale and high morale drives exceptional performance. High morale is the single most powerful motivation - even above financial - that drives exceptional performance on a team.

An effective foundation of common objectives can be broken down into eight essential elements.

Vision

A vision statement expresses a measurable ideal for the organization to reach at some point in the future - where you are going. These ideals become the passion for the team and the employees. Try to identify objectives the employees would boast about achieving, ones that inspire "*esprit de corps*." A classic vision statement once came from JFK when he said "We will put a man on the moon in a decade." All good Technical Marketeers have vision and know how to articulate it.

Values

Values are the basic virtues, the ethical backbone of the company's daily actions, for everyone working in the organization. Values are real issues employees can feel, believe, see, understand, and commit to. Grab onto some virtues that employees can hold true to, and that are necessary for the team to operate effectively. Examples include honesty, integrity, self-discipline, high customer satisfaction, and high productivity levels.

Mission

A statement expressing the value proposition the business delivers to its clients in the simplest, basic form. It is the answer to "What is in it for the customer?"

Motivation

It is easy to motivate yourself, not easy to motivate your team. It is the "*ownership of responsibility to achieve their own results*" that unleashes initiative and provides satisfaction and achievement. This is the fireball that produces outstanding results for the organization. It must be set forth initially and maintained regularly to compete and succeed - as long as you have star players.

Business Plan

A document containing the detailed plans for executing the mission and the vision: the management team, organization structure, financial plans, competition assessment, market differentiation, and product or service descriptions.

Marketing Plan

A document containing the detailed plans for creating the demand and producing sales for the products and services offered by the organization. Be sure to include Technical Marketing plans.

Goals and Responsibilities

A series of documents that establish the goals and responsibilities for each person in the organization, the results and deliverables expected, a timeframe for delivery, guidelines they are to work within, and resources they are to utilize.

These must be reviewed on a regular basis because of the nature of change in business. To be successful, the organization must reinforce each employee in knowing their own goals, responsibilities and deliverables and working to achieve them. The organization must reward them for exceptional performance. Like the business plan, goals and responsibilities are an active plan of attack.

Many organizations have adopted the S.M.A.R.T. goals system and there is online tracking software that measures employees performance based on this. Goals must be Specific, Measurable, Attainable, Realistic and Timely. Using S.M.A.R.T. makes goal achievement powerful. Do yourself a favor and keep these short and sweet. One page maximum.

Organization Plan

A plan that allows the staff to understand the steps and processes in the organization - displaying what happens before and after each employees involvement.

As with the other elements of the foundation, the organization plan must be known and understood by every employee in the organization to ensure effective execution of procedures in their own area. But to be really efficient try to keep this to one page per initiave. Developing a 200 page business plan is only going to produce a 200 page business plan. People that know what they are doing, do get started this way. Business plans might be good for when you need really big investors, so they can understand their risk. For you high performance team, keep it high performance, limit the amount of documentation you keep.

Operating Protocol

Identifies the actions required to ensure the foundation is continuously communicated, reviewed and updated as needed. Operating protocol assures the focus of the organization is expressed frequently throughout. This helps to ensure that each employee knows and understands the foundation.

14

Certifications

Certifications have great educational value. I have taken many certification courses and passed many tests. I previously developed the opinion that certifications were a waste of time, and just another marketing gimmick.

I've changed my mind ever so slightly. Certifications have great education value. The process of studying for them, then taking the exams, it all has great education value that will help your career advance. Although there isn't a Technical Marketing Certification ... yet. Its ok if you just read the books and don't take the tests. I have spent a ton of time and money on certifications, and I have a lot of them. But in reality, at the end of the day, certifications don't matter to a Technical Marketeer. Yet. Truth be known, many of the "Certified Experts" that I know only have big ego's and they can't be used for Technical Marketing. And when it comes to real problem solving, "Certified Experts" will be of only marginal use if any at all.

Unfortunately, certifications have evolved into another method to get people brainwashed on a certain company's product at the consumer's expense of time and money. For Technical Marketeer's, unless it is a way to gain Technical Marketing advantage or part of your competitive analysis, it is a waste to channel your time and money in that direction. Certifications might be good for support and IT professionals, yet not so much for Technical Marketeers.

If a product is so complex that it takes umpteen levels of certification, thousands of dollars to support it, your own money to pay for the certification, your own money to buy the equipment and books to educate yourself, along with a big ego and the correct alignment of the stars and planets to keep it running, it isn't worthy of today's fast and lean datacenters, nor your time. If you see a company that has a product with a big certification program, I advise you to question it's value to your cause.

Users are smart enough to figure things out. If a product isn't easy enough to use, the marketplace will reject it. Products are easier to use now such that it only takes 3 clicks to get a product up and running. Get the product installed, running, document it and move on. If you don't, or if you can't, the war will be fought and won by the time you poke your head out of the lab.

Certifications actually distract raw talent away from the development of brilliant ideas for companies. Technical Marketing ideas. Certifications result in a reduction in GDP and contribute to a decline in the economy.

Unfortunately, certifications expire, unlike a college education. The companies that issue them can and will take them away from you, the tests become devalued as they are sold on the internet anyway, they are temporary, they have minimal value on your resume and they don't have the accreditation as that of real universities and colleges. If you do go down the path of certifications, and they expire, don't bother re-certifying. That is even more foolish effort designed only to generate more money for the issuing organization. Get it, post it on your resume, or online profile and move on.

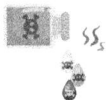

15
SEO

What is SEO?

Search Engine Optimization (SEO), is the digital marketing strategy of boosting the number of customers and potential customers that visit your website. It is all about eyeballs. Getting more eyeballs to see your stuff. Your marketing messages, your products, anything you want the mass of the globe to know about. It is also about improving the quality of the visitors to your website. By quality, we mean potential customers that you have a real shot of converting into regular patrons of your business. Sound SEO strategies increase the exposure to your brand in the digital world by using what is known as organic online marketing tactics.

Organic?

No, not the way we use organic to describe certain types of food. We mean attracting customers by using digital marketing strategies that do not cost you a dime.

If you're like me, when you do a search engine search, i.e. google. com, you don't look at the top 1 -5 responses that say "ad" next to them, because you know someone paid money for you to look at those links. Those ad's are NOT organic, they are paid. I want the truth, the real response not influenced by paid search results. I always scroll down to the first three entries that shows up below the ad's. This is called the coveted "3-pack". That is where the organic search results appear. I understand search engines have to make some money, but that goes against why search engines are supposed to exist to begin with. Sorry, that is a different topic for another time.

There are two ways to attract visitors to your website: paid and non-paid or organic. An example of paid online advertising is called pay per click, or PPC. Every time someone clicks on an ad you have paid to have displayed online, you have to pay a fee to enjoy the increase in website traffic. With an organic online marketing strategy such as SEO, you do not have to pay for an increase in website traffic.

Although the term SEO refers to search engines, it really boils down to knowing what potential customers are looking for when they use a search engine to find a product or a service that you offer. It really boils down to knowing the search engine's algorithm's.

You can view search engines as digital answering machines. At blazing fast speeds, they cover the entire Internet to discover which content matches individual searches. It's just that search engines "cache" or store search results in a way that makes them retrievable at extremely fast speeds.

Think about the online searches you perform. You type in a word or phrase to find a product or learn more about something that piques your interest. After hitting 'enter" you receive a list of websites that the search engine had concluded best match your search words. The search engine is doing a "look ahead" into the database into what it thinks your best match would be. It sort of tries to do some of the thinking for you in a sense.

As a business owner, your goal is to have your SEO strategy land you on the first page right under the paid ad's. Preferably as one of the first three websites listed.

The technical marketing relationship with SEO involves analyzing the data generated from the competitive analysis you conducted to help develop the most effective SEO strategy.

The vast majority of Internet traffic is sent to websites through organic searches. The rest of this chapter discusses the basics of SEO and how to use it to boost your business presence online.

The Importance of SEO

Do you really need a SEO strategy to attract more customers to your business? Unless you have developed the patent for a customer magnet, the answer is a resounding yes.

Here's why.

Your Website Traffic Depends on Organic Searches

There's that term organic again. As we know, organic searches refer to website traffic that businesses get because of online searches performed through Google, Bing, and Yahoo. Since google drives about 75% of all searches, for the sake of simplicity, we will refer to the search engine giant when discussing organic online searches. Getting your website noticed on Google goes a long way towards pushing your products and services ahead of the competition.

Earn Trust by Building Credibility

If your business ranks high in Google searches, you can expect your brand to become one of the authorities in your product and/or service niches. Customer prospects that find you in the top half of the first search results page will help you gain instant credibility. With credibility comes more visits and more time spent by your potential customers on your business website, which eventually will help you earn the level of trust that leads to more sales.

A Huge Wheel in the Buying Cycle

The buying cycle starts with research and more than ever, customers are spending plenty of time online researching products and companies before handing over their credit card information. SEO can help your business educate customers by offering information your customers cannot find anywhere else online. We mentioned trust and credibility. One way to earn trust by building credibility is using SEO to help customer learn more about your business.

Affordable Marketing Strategy

Like other marketing strategies, SEO costs money. However, SEO is one of the most affordable ways to attract more customers. Consider SEO as an investment, not an expense on the company income statement. If done right, you can earn one of the highest returns on a marketing investment.

Not a One and Done Strategy

Although you want to get as much out of SEO as soon as possible, you should look at it as a long term strategy that can have a positive impact for several years to come. You might have to tweak content to adjust to ever changing business terms, as well as update links, but the foundation of your SEO strategy will deliver long term results. No other marketing strategy has a similar staying power.

Mystery Solved: How Search Engines Work

The big three search engines-Google, Bing, and Yahoo- have three important functions.

- Crawl
- Index
- Rank

Crawling means the big three search engines deploy a virtual spider to cover the entire Internet for specified content. Search engine spiders retain the code and content of a website, before sending the information back to a search engine server.

Note:

You probably don't know this but internet web crawlers have been around as long as the Internet. Before Google, Yahoo and Bing existed, companies like Alta Vista and Webcrawler were the search engine kings.

Indexing represents the process of storing and organizing the code and content obtained by the search engine spider. After indexing a web page, the page is then eligible to be compared to other web pages that were found using similar searches.

The final piece of the search engine puzzle is rank. Search engine ranking means rating each web page ordered by a search from the most relevant to the least relevant.

Note:

Google didn't invent their "Ranking" algorithm, they "borrowed it". An entrepreneur in Florida actually came up with the idea of "ranking" results, and a Google board member took the idea and implemented it.

How does SEO play a role in how search engines work? The answer lies in the meaning of the acronym - Search Engine Optimization.

SEO is a digital marketing strategy that tries to get search engine crawlers to retrieve the most relevant content that is first indexed, before it undergoes the ranking process. A successful SEO strategy ensures every crawler retrieves the information the web page wants to present. For example, to attract the attention of a Google spider, your SEO strategy might be to strategically integrate the right keywords into the content of the web page.

Search engines might seem like a mystery. However, the mystery lies in the ever changing algorithms that calculate the quality of the content uploaded to a web page. Google's search engine ranking algorithms, which seem to change monthly, leave many webmasters scratching their heads. This can be frustrating if you are trying to design strategies that stand the test of time, so you can spend time focusing on your business instead of SEO.

To avoid making SEO too complicated, the following SEO techniques remain time tested techniques the algorithms devised by the big three search engines use to crawl, index, and rank web pages.

An Overview of Keyword Research

The key to ranking high in the three major search engines is to perform keyword research. Does this involve some high tech procedure that requires a Ph.D? No it doesn't, and you do not have to spend much time discovering how your customers find you online.

Keyword research just requires you to know your target market thoroughly, such as learning how they find businesses like yours in cyberspace.

You need to answer three important questions to perform keyword research:

- What are your customers looking for in a product and/or service?
- How many customers are searching for businesses like yours online?
- How do your customers want the search results presented?

Long before you implement SEO strategies such as keyword research, you must identify your customer base, as well as their buying needs.

How to Perform Keyword Research

Put yourself in the shoes of your customers. How would you find a business like yours online? Let's use a pizzeria as an example. Here are a few possible keywords, depending on the type of pizza the restaurant specializes in making:

- Thin Crust Pizza
- Deep Dish Pizza
- Gluten Free pizza
- Meat Lover's Pizza
- New York Style Pizza

As you can see, these are five logical options for potential customers to use as keywords to find the best pizzeria. However, you know there are far more keywords to describe your business.

Luckily, you can perform more intensive keyword researches by using a keyword research tool. You enter the keywords you have into one of the best keyword research tools.

https://backlinko.com/keyword-research-tools

The keyword research tool you decide to use will present similar keywords and the average volume of monthly searches people have performed against those keywords. With the average volume of monthly searches, you will discover which of your keywords are the most popular among the members of your target market.

Keyword research can also open the door to other possible topics for your website content.

Note:

Understand the difference between low competition and high competition keywords. Although both types of keywords can increase traffic to your website, low competition keywords are more effective in giving your website a competitive advantage. Low competition keywords are words and phrases that your customers input into search engines, but the words and phrases are not used by many of your competitors. When a customer types in a low competition keyword into a search engine, your business has a much better chance of ranking on the first page of a search engine result. In terms of competition this is a good strategy to look for.

The Components of Technical SEO

Although the three major search engines place a strong emphasis on creating helpful original content that contains the proper keywords, Google, Bing, and Yahoo also stress the importance of including several technical website attributes. Hence, we have the term technical SEO, which is not to be confused with the topic of this book, technical marketing

There are the four main components of technical SEO:

Secure Sockets Layer (SSL)

Sounds like an underground cable term, but SSL refers to website security technology that produces an encrypted code for keeping sensitive data secure. It is easy to notice whether a website uses the SSL security protocol. Look for URLs that begin with "https://, instead of the insecure start to an URL of "http://. Google announced the importance of SSL in 2014 and Bing and Yahoo quickly followed Google's lead. All you have to do is install an SSL certificate on your website.

https://letsencrypt.org/

Make Your Website Quick to Load

Nothing turns off a visitor to a website more than having to wait for content to load. We do not live in the age of dial up Internet technology anymore, which means it is imperative for your website to upload at least as fast as the fastest websites in your business niche. All three of the powerful search engines consider page upload speeds important for ranking websites.

Studies have been performed and found that visitors to a webpage on a laptop or workstation will abandon the site after 3 seconds. Similar studies have found the average abandonment time for mobile devices is 2 seconds. Something needs to happen within that time frame or you lose your customer, sometimes forever.

Here are a few tips to increase the speed of your web page uploads:
- Choose a web host that delivers fast web page uploads
- Work with a fast domain system (DSM) provider
- Minimize the use of scripts and plugins
- Insert small images
- Compress your web pages
- Simplify the website's programming code

Here are some tools to help you identify where your web page needs help, and how fast it loads:
- https://gtmetrix.com/
- https://www.webpagetest.org/
- https://tools.pingdom.com/

Choosing your website content management system can have an effect. I love Wordpress and build all of my site's using Wordpress. However, Wordpress is becoming "fat ware", which means its bloated with plugins and features and so much extra unnecessary stuff that as a content management system, it can slow down your website. There are other content management tools and frameworks, such as Joomla, so it would be wise to at least investigate these additional frameworks.

If you don't want to mess with all of that, or you just don't have a clue and don't want to, you can hire developers that know those frameworks to do the work for you at relatively low prices. You can also find SEO experts in these sites.

A couple of places to look for this type of talent:

- https://www.upwork.com
- https://www.freelancer.com

Going Mobile

Your customers are making more purchases on the move. Think about the pizzeria example mentioned above. Mobile phones have given us the capability to order a meat lover's pizza from virtually anywhere. However, far too many websites are not considered "mobile friendly" by the big three search engines, and that is a bad thing. Google has introduced a "mobile first" approach to indexing content, which means your website must be designed to read and navigate easily on a mobile communication device. Make sure your business website is completely responsive for tablet, laptop, mobile, and desktop users.

Add an XML Sitemap

An XML sitemap represents a file that makes sure the big three search engines understand what is on your website. Think of an XML sitemap as you think of a road map. An XML sitemap tells Google, Bing, and Yahoo exactly where each page is located on your business website. It also informs the big three search engines when you last modified a web page, as well as how often you update each page. Some of the content management systems, such as Wordpress, have a plugin that automatically does this for you when you change something or post a new blog post.

Know about Robots

Robots.txt files have been around since the invention of the Internet. The robots.txt file is, well, a text file. It's sole purpose it to tell robots, or web crawlers, or the Google bot, which parts of your website that you want to "allow" them to crawl. It can also tell the bot scrapers which parts of your website you "don't allow" or don't want your content ending up in the search engine caches. For example, you could conceivably create a robots.txt file that disallows all search engines from crawling and caching

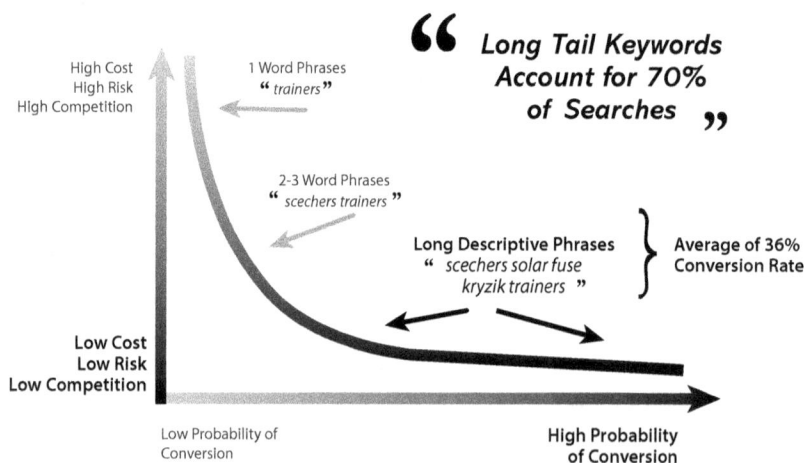

High Cost
High Risk
High Competition

1 Word Phrases
" *trainers* "

" *Long Tail Keywords Account for 70% of Searches* **"**

2-3 Word Phrases
" *scechers trainers* "

Long Descriptive Phrases
" *scechers solar fuse kryzik trainers* "

Average of 36% Conversion Rate

Low Cost
Low Risk
Low Competition

Low Probability of Conversion

High Probability of Conversion

your website. If you need customers to find you, this is bad. If you want to keep your website hidden, this is good. If you want only parts of your website to be crawled and cached, then the robots.txt is where you do this.

http://www.robotstxt.org/

Short tail vs. Long tail

Now there is the concept of short tail vs. long tail searches. Think about how your customer tries to find you. Do they simply look for "Pepperoni Pizza" or do they look for "Pepperoni Pizza New York Style? A search for just Pepperoni Pizza is a short tail search because contains only a short 2-3 work phrase. A search for Pepperoni Pizza New York Style is a long tail search because it contains more than 3 words in the phrase. Short tail words and phrases cost more because there are a ton of competitors using the same words. Short tail words and phrases are high cost, highly competitive and have a lower probability of conversion into a sale. Long tail words and phrases are lower cost, not very competitive and have a higher probability of conversion into a sale. Long tail searches account for about 70% of searches, so it behooves you to spend some time looking at what long tail searches your customers will be using to find you.

The Importance of Link Building

Let's say you have uploaded the type of content you think the visitors to your website want to read. By integrating the right keywords in the right places, you improved the ranking of your website in the three major search engines. Now, you have to build on your hard work by linking to other authority websites and in return, having the same websites link back to your business website. This is called link building, and unfortunately is viewed highly in search engine algorithm's.

Think of it like this, the more people you know that say you are a good person, the more popular you are. Those people are "links" in the search algorithm paradigm. This is why you see so many people linking their website profile to the Facebook profile, and try to get people to comment and like back, comment on your website, etc. Search engines use this massive globe of interconnected "links" to rate your popularity. It's not the only thing, but it does count.

The more Google's mysterious search engine algorithm changes, the more it stays the same. For example, links have always been a vital measuring stick for Google when it comes to ranking web pages. Websites that present helpful information typically link to websites that follow the same helpful content strategy. You have two different types of links to understand:

- Inbound
- Internal

Inbound links take website visitors from one web page to another web page uploaded by another webmaster. The more quality inbound links you have, the more credibility Google will give you in the search engine rankings. Look at inbound links in the same way politicians look for votes, except, you do not have to pay for high quality inbound links.

Internal links direct visitors to your website to other web pages you have uploaded on the same site. A large number of internal links that direct visitors to the same page alerts Google that the page is an important component of your content strategy. The key is not to create too many internal links to the same page.

How do you acquire more inbound links? You can acquire links to website naturally when other websites link to your content because it is helpful and it builds trust with readers. The main reason you receive traffic because of links comes from the high quality content you upload that other people want to use as a resource or reference. Naturally earned links requires no effort on your part, except for creating useful, original content that helps visitors to your website solve problems.

Establishing what is referred to as a healthy link profile lets the big three search engines know you are acquiring links and building trust fairly. Although one of more competitors might pay for links, you should stick with the old school way of adding links by focusing on your content marketing strategy the hard way, by earning it.

SEO and Content Marketing

Content marketing represents an online marketing strategy that has only recently become an integral part of a plan to generate more customer leads. You write website content that is targeted to the audience you want to reach. For example, if you run an automotive repair business, your website content should be mostly about ways your customers can improve the performance of their vehicles.

At the heart of content marketing is the building of trust we have mentioned before in this chapter. Content marketing is all about gaining credibility with your target audience, which eventually can lead to an increase in sales. The content marketing strategy is also used by business owners that want customers to download an eBook or sign up for a free initial consultation.

The primary objective of any content marketing program is to develop long-term relationships with customers by demonstrating you are the authority in your business niche. You must upload useful content for your target audience. Then, you need to promote the content by getting it on the screens used by your target audience.

How Does SEO Fit into Content Marketing?

Although SEO and content marketing are two different ways to get noticed online, the two strategies work seamlessly together to boost your search engine rankings. Here's how you use SEO to work with your content marketing program:

- Discover and research your target audience
- Perform accurate keyword research
- Upload helpful content that builds trust
- Update content on a regular basis

How do you write helpful content that builds trust? You have to present well-written content that contains no grammar or spelling errors. Nothing loses you credibility faster than creating content that looks as if it was written by a first grader. If writing is not in your wheelhouse, hire someone that has established a record of writing high quality website content. Make sure to add examples of the points you make to boost your credibility. Write for your target audience and maybe most important of all, ensure your content is easy to read.

We've All Gone Local

According to Google, nearly 50% of all online searches are performed with a "local intent." The importance of local searches is apparent when you search for a business, without typing in the location of the business.

Take the computers hooked up at the local library. When you search for a nearby grocery, google will return a list of businesses located close to the library.

Standard online searches use keywords such as "How to rotate car tires." A local search will read something like "Affordable Dentists in Atlanta." What do local searches have to do with SEO? The answer is a recently introduced digital marketing strategy called local SEO.

Local SEO represents a highly effective strategy to market your business online to local customers. It allows businesses to market products and services locally at the exact times customers are searching for the same products and services in cyberspace.

The main goal for your business is to become part of that "3-pack" of organic search results that appears after a customer performs a local search. To become part of the coveted 3-pack, you must join the rapidly growing list of businesses that are a part of Google My Business.

Here are the three most important criteria used for churning out local search engine results:

- The closeness of a customer to your business
- The relevance of the search to your products and services
- Feedback from customers that have bought your products and services

An Overview of Google My Business

If you have ever opted out of listing your home's landline in the White Pages, you know the omission makes it difficult for long lost friends to find you. Sure, they can perform an online search to find you, but many of the listings are significantly outdated.

The same principle applies to your business and Google My Business.

Note: Keep in mind, that if your business is run solely online and you're customers are global, then this section may not apply to you. Virtual or online businesses are not allowed on Google My Business, as of the time of this writing. Apparently, not having a Google My Business won't hurt your virtual or online business.

Known in the past as Google+ and Google local, Google My Business is the place where you create your business profile. First, you claim a Google My Business listing, and then you complete the profile by submitting accurate and up to date information.

In addition to listing your business name, address, and phone number, you also present your business description, the list of services offered, and the times of operation. With Google My Business, the more information you submit, the more likely your business will appear in the "3-pack" of local searches.

A huge part of implementing a successful local SEO program is to ensure your Google My Business profile is 100% accurate. Any deviation for the information you present in your Google My Business profile with your business listings in other online directories will penalize you in local searches. Almost 70% of consumers polled in a survey stated they would not buy from a business that had inaccurate information in any of the online business directories.

Unlike technical SEO, local SEO is all about spending a little time creating accurate and up to date business profiles online.

Measuring the Success of SEO Strategies

If you do not measure the success of your SEO strategy, you will never know the impact your business has on search engine rankings. Professionals specializing in offering SEO consulting services monitor a large number of metrics to help clients improve their SEO strategies. Now that most everything is online, we have so many tools to help us find buyers for our products and services. I remember the days when a billboard would have an ad placed on it. How did that advertiser know how many sales were a result of that billboard? They didn't. With SEO, you can have this information at your fingertips.

Conversion Rate

Take the number of conversions and divide that by the number of unique website visits to calculate the conversion rate of a web page. You can measure the conversion rate for an email newsletter sign up campaign, as well as for the purchase of a specific product. Conversion rates are perfect for helping business owners determine the return on investment for different SEO strategies.

Pages per Visit

When you attract a customer or potential customer to your business website, you want the visitor to your website to visit more than one web page. Pages per visit lets you know the average number of pages each visitor to your website clicks. It represents an important SEO metric that ultimately determines the direction of your content marketing program, because it tells you where your customers are going and where they want to go.

Time on Page

How long do your website visitors spend on each of your web pages. Duration often indicates the quality of a web page. For example, a 1,000-word article that readers average about 15 seconds on is not doing a good job of generating enough interest for visitors to the web page to keep on reading. You have to factor in the purpose of a web page. For example, "About Us" pages should have a lower time on page number than a page that describes several of your products and services.

Bounce Rate

For SEO, bounce means a website visitor has left a website. A high bounce rate for a web page can mean a number of things, from poor content to the lack of visual appeal, to slow load time. Look at your business web page bounce rates like restaurant owners look at customer feedback cards. Moreover, take into account the bounce rate for the home page, the place where visitors spend little time getting the information they need most. If you have a lot of bounces and fast bounces, it means your visitors aren't the right ones, or your page is not visually compelling, or not even visually appealing.

Search Traffic

Although search rankings are a vital SEO measuring stick, the metric itself is not enough to learn about the effectiveness of your business SEO strategy. You can rank high in Google's search engine, but not receive the amount of traffic you expect from such a high ranking. By using the Google Analytics tool, you will uncover website traffic data that will help you change your SEO campaign, if needed.

DIY or Hire an Expert?

The purpose of this chapter is to give you an overview of SEO. By using a broad brush, we should have given you an idea about the importance of SEO, as well as insight into how to increase the number of high quality links and take advantage of Google My Business to rank your business high in local searches.

Can you implement an SEO strategy on your own? Well, you do not have to hold a Ph.D to build links or even present fresh, useful content that helps your customers solve problems. However, for technical SEO issues such as making your website mobile friendly, you should consider working with a professional that specializes in offering top rated SEO services.

Do You Have the Time?

Business owners typically have a large number of tasks to juggle at the same time. Most time-strapped business owners do not have the time to handle SEO responsibilities. Let's look at a few SEO-related tasks you can expect to perform each month if you decide to handle the SEO campaign yourself.

- Between four and eight blog posts
- Anywhere from 50 to 250 social media posts
- •wo email newsletters

This is just your content marketing obligations. Other SEO tasks you would have to perform include local SEO information management and continuous link analysis. Do not forget the analytics you must perform to understand how your SEO strategy is faring against the competition.

The Value of an SEO Expert

With limited time available for SEO, most small business owners should consider going with an SEO specialist. An SEO agency is an even better option, as the team oriented approach the agency takes can help you accomplish more SEO-related tasks. However, you must consider the impact that hiring an SEO expert or agency will have on your budget. SEO professional services are not cheap, but the return on your investment can far exceed the amount of money you spend to work with an SEO expert.

How to Choose the Best SEO Expert

You should be able to access online reviews and ratings from websites like Yelp and the Better Business Bureau (BBB). The question is what criteria should you use to vet and ultimately select the right SEO expert (s)?

- Client references
- Case study examples
- Approach to link building
- When will I start to see an uptick in customer leads?
- Have you provided SEO services for a business like mine?
- How much do your services cost?

SEO is not a digital marketing strategy that you can tinker with as you go along. In fact, you often need to get SEO strategies right the first time, especially for technical SEO services.

Some online places to find SEO and Content Marketing Experts, again: https://www.upwork.com, https://www.freelancer.com

16
Blogging For Business

Business owners have several digital marketing tools literally at their fingertips. From uploading "How to…" videos to making websites technically appropriate for SEO purposes, you can get a leg up on the competition. Yet, there is one strategy that often flies under the radar.

It's called blogging for business.

Just the word "blogging" makes many business owners and operators feel a bit uneasy. It shouldn't.

Blogging for business is just one element of a powerful content marketing program.

Overview of Content Marketing

Content marketing has gained momentum over the past few years in the world of online marketing, and it should. All three of the major search engines place more ranking power on content than just about any other search engine ranking factor. So, what exactly is content marketing?

Content marketing is all about sharing information. It represents a highly effective way to spread the word about your business by sharing useful information your readers need to solve problems. The information can be educational, such as explaining how to rotate four tires. It can also be entertaining, as in the form of a video that captivates viewers by using comedy or drama to share a message.

Content marketing is not about making hard sales pitches that often turn off consumers. The same principle applies to blogging for business.

The best explanation of content marketing comes from the Content Marketing Institute:

> **"** *Content Marketing's purpose is to attract and retain customers by consistently creating and curating relevant and valuable content with the intention of changing or enhancing consumer behavior. It is an ongoing process that is best integrated into your overall marketing strategy, and it focuses on owning media, not renting it.* **"**

ROI for Content Marketing

Return on investment results for content marketing programs vary depending on the size of a program, as well as how long a content marketing program is in place. Nonetheless, data demonstrates content marketing delivers a strong ROI on your company's marketing dollars. Here are some things we've learned.

- Costs 62% less than the cost of standard marketing practices
- Produces three times as many leads as the leads generated by paid searches
- Converts six times more customer prospects than the customer prospects converted by traditional marketing methods

Just under one percent of business leads result in sales. Content marketing, and in particular blogging for business, is developed to increase the customer conversion rate substantially.

Blogging Should be the Focus of your Business Content Marketing Strategy

When you look at the food pyramid, you will notice a foundation of foods and servings that are essential to our well-being. Blogging is our foundation for the content marketing pyramid. Sure, it's sexier to send pithy tweets and upload hilarious photos and memes. (yes, photos are considered content). However, blogging for business is how you get your products and services on the digital map.

Blog posts are the pioneers of content marketing because of the useful information they convey. Blogging for your business makes you come across as an expert in your niche. Because of your helpful information, visitors return to your blog regularly to see what you have up your content sleeve. Sharing relevant information with the visitors to your blog builds credibility for your business, and you know what they say about credibility. It builds trust, and what does trust do for your business? It leads to more sales.

Benefits of Blogging on a Business Website

Do you really need to contribute to a blog to get more recognition for your business? The answer is a resounding yes, and here are 8 reasons why blogging for business is a good idea.

More Search Engine Traffic

When you look at the three big search engines, look at them like you look at a large pond stocked full of fish. The more lines you cast into the pond, the more likely you will catch fish. Now, what does that have to do with blogging for business, you might be asking.

The more content you upload to your business blog, the more web pages carrying your domain will be indexed in the Google, Bing, and Yahoo search engines. Every new blog post you upload to your website is like dropping another hook into the large search engine pond.

Perfect Complement for Social Media

Social media for business is much more than posting vacation photos. It's all about content as well. With a business blog that you consistently contribute content, you bolster your social media presence. Use social media networks like Twitter and Facebook to direct customer prospects to the content presented in your website blog. Share links to blog posts; enjoy a strong uptick to the number of website visitors.

Attracts More Leads

Research performed by several of online marketing specialists indicates businesses attract more leads because of the uploading of more content. According to content marketing leader Hubspot, businesses with between 401 and 1,000 pages of content receive six times more leads than businesses that present between 51 and 100 pages of content. Think about this: More blog posts equal more price quote requests, more contact form submissions, and more email opt-in agreements.

Higher Conversion Rates

The ultimate goal of any digital marketing strategy is to convert interested consumers into lifelong patrons of your business. When you establish your business as the authority in your operating niche, you will see your conversion rates increase. Blogging for business that delivers high-quality content will also build a large base of loyal readers that eventually turn into regular customers.

Add More Inbound Links

The more Google's famous search engine ranking algorithm changes, the more it stays the same. At least it stays the same in regards to the importance of inbound links. Long a vital component of search engine ranking criteria, adding more inbound links remains at the top of the must do list for Internet marketers. If you do not have a business blog, you are losing a prime opportunity to add more inbound links from authoritative websites.

The Human Touch

Your home page or about page on your website will not show the personal side of your business as well as blog posts can deliver the human touch. The digital era has kind of sterilized relationships because of a decrease in personal interactions. Blogging for business allows you to reveal information that conveys your passion for certain topics.

Encourages Insightful Discussions

Outside of Facebook, perhaps no other digital marketing tool gets you closer to your customers than blogging for business. In addition to providing a section for reader feedback, you can also get a heartbeat about how your readers feel by receiving emails through the business website contact page. Learning what your customers think is a vital tool to have for improving your products and services.

Fresh Content Rules on Google

There is no doubt Google rewards fresh website content that provides useful information. Contributing to a blog on a consistent basis ensures your website is uploading fresh content.

Of course, more content also means more opportunities to receive inbound links.

Tips for Business Blogging

Content marketing, such as blogging for business, represents a powerful tool to increase exposure for your products and services. However, there are a few tips that can turn your business blog into one of the most popular web pages in your operating niche.

Helpful and Relevant Content

As we have mentioned before, uploading useful, relevant content that helps readers solve problems is a proven method for increasing the level of credibility required to build trust. One of the principles to follow for presenting helpful content is to show, not just tell. In other words, provide real life examples of how and why a certain business solution works.

Solicit Feedback

Encourage your readers to leave feedback, and not just feedback that responds to your posts. You are interested in learning about fresh ways to improve your business operations.

Make sure to acknowledge reader feedback by leaving a comment for them or sending them personalized emails.

Follow a Content Schedule

Although there is not a clearly defined scheduled for posting business blogs, you should create and consistently follow a content schedule. The benefit of following a content schedule is your readers will know exactly when you will upload the next post. Like for your products and services, consistency is a vital element of blogging for business.

Focus on Your Niche

Most business blogs should focus on a narrow list of topics to ensure the message conveyed reaches the right target audience. For example, if you write a blog for a hardware store, you want to avoid writing about topics that have nothing to do with the tools, equipment, and appliances your store offers.

Point of View Matters

Devoted readers of your blog want to know how you feel about the products and services that are available in your operating mix. An electronics store owner can blog about the latest Smartphone technology or a sporting goods store owner can write about the latest waterproof technology for backpacks and camping gear.

Change Up Format

We are not talking about changing how each post appears, although you can tinker with the design of your blog. Changing up the format is all about changing the amount of words you present in your posts, as well as how you arrange the content on each page. You can write a 2,000 post one week that describes organic farming and then upload a video the next week that demonstrates one or more organic farming techniques.

Should Be Easy to Read

Long winded paragraphs combined with using overly complex words is a great way to alienate your target audience. Readers want short, clearly written content mixed in with a few numbered and bullet point lists. The key is to capture the attention of your readers, not lull them into sleep.

Go the Freelance Route

If writing is not your thing, there are a countless number of freelance writers out there that can take your talking points and make them sing to your target audience. In addition, working with a freelance editor ensures you have a fresh set of eyes to review your content.

Subscription Should Be Easy to Do

Having your readers subscribe to your blog or at least receive notices whenever you upload a post requires some type of digital form that allows them to opt-in. The key is to place the opt-in form in an easy to see place on your business website. For instance, you can place the opt-in form on the left upper side of the home page to make it the first thing readers see when they access your website.

Promote, Promote, and Promote

This is not about shamelessly promoting your business blog in every comment you post online. It is all about offering useful information on message boards and comment sections for a period, before adding your blog URL, website URL, and business name under your first and last name. The best way to turn off potential readers is to link frequently back to your blog. Give them a more subtle hint about what you have to offer in the form of relevant content.

Finally, remember it will take a little time for you to build the type of momentum you need to gain plenty of subscribers for your blog. Follow the adage "Slow and easy wins the race," and you should have a successful business blog that will be the envy of your competitors.

How to Create a Business Blogging Plan

Like anything else in business, you have to come up with a plan for your blog. Uploading content that represents your business reputation is much too important for you to simply wing it. You need to devise a carefully crafted plan to deliver the greatest return on both your time and money investments.

Let's go over some common planning steps that will help you create a popular blog for your business.

Develop a Mission Statement

Your blogging plan needs a steering mechanism, and that comes in the form of a well-thought out mission statement. Content Marketing Institute member, Joe Pulizzi says there is a three-part process involved in devising a blogging for business mission statement. "The why must come before the what," he said. For the why answer, you should answer each of these questions:

- What is your target audience?
- What do you want to accomplish for your target audience?
- What type of content will you present to your target audience?

By type of content, will you present advice, helpful tips, success stories, and new solutions for common problems?

Even better, you can mix it up and present different types of content to keep your target audience engaged with your business blog.

Read Other Business Blogs in Your Niche

The goal here is not to mimic what a competitor is doing with a blog, but learning about how different business bloggers approach running their blogs. Moreover, you will also learn more about what are the hot button topics in your operating niche. You will discover what a blog you like to read does right, as well as what a blog you dislike does wrong. Make sure any blog you read before embarking on your blogging for business journey has been online for at least one year.

Select the Blog Content Categories

At this stage of the planning game, you should have a clear understanding as to why your business blog is online, as well as which readers it will help solve problems and how the blog will improve your business operation.

Now is the time to select between five and 10 content categories that discuss topics that are relevant in your business niche. Let's look at how a sporting goods store owner could choose content categories:

- Camping gear
- Firearms
- Fishing equipment
- Soccer apparel
- Basketball shoes
- Cycling accessories

This is not an exclusive list, just one list to give you an idea that content categories can produce numerous topics. The topics available for the firearms category are seemingly endless.

Your blog should read like a trade publication, with the primary difference being you will inject humor and personal anecdotes into your business blog content. Stick with the initial list of categories for up to one year, and then reevaluate the list to add more categories or take off a category or two because of over exposure.

Establish the Blogging Schedule

We have already discussed the importance of creating a reasonable blogging for business schedule. By reasonable, we mean a reasonable amount of content that does not overwhelm the subscribers to your blog.

First, decide on how many posts you want to upload each month. Remember the goal is to offer quality content, not overload your readers with information they do not need. A sound content scheduling strategy is to upload one blog post per week. You also have to decide on the length of each post and as we mentioned, variety is the spice of life when it comes to blogging for business.

Second, if you opt for a weekly blog post, choose the day when you release the post. Monday and Friday typically are not the best days. Choose Tuesday, Wednesday, or Thursday to allow your readers a little time to settle into their routines during the week, as well as not have their focus 100% on the weekend.

Finally, and perhaps most important, make sure you stay consistent with your blog post output and the day when your readers can expect to read your brilliant insights.

Analyze Blogging for Business Results

You might have heard why it is important to measure and analyze the importance of your business website. Google Analytics does a great job of keeping business owners apprised about a number of website performance factors. The same principle applies to blogging for business, as the only way to learn if your blog is making a positive impact is to determine whether you are meeting your business goals.

Here are the four best blogging analytic tools in 2019:

- Google Analytics
- Momently
- Clicky
- Matomo

The metrics you use to analyze the business blog differ a little bit from the metrics used to measure the success of your website. All four analytic tools provide step-by step instructions to ensure you get the most out of each tool.

Best Business Blogs

Cyberspace offers a seemingly infinite number of resources to help business owners develop world class blogs. However, blogging for business resources do not have to be solely an exercise in technical explanations. There are eight sites out there that by simply reading the content and reviewing how the sites are set up for blogs, you should come away with a blogging for business plan that will be the envy of every operator in your niche.

- Forbes: Entrepreneurs
- Mashable
- Fast Company
- Chris Brogan
- Tech Crunch
- Venture Beat
- Marketing Profs: Small Business
- Duct Tape Marketing

With these resource at your fingertips, you will stay current on the hot button topics in the world of business to keep your blogging for business posts attracting new readers every week.

17

Social Media Marketing

Connect with your Customers

If you are like the billions of people around the world, you spend at least a little time each day cultivating friendships on social media networking sites. You might reach out to a like-minded professional on LinkedIn who lives half the world away or you might connect with someone who has the same devotion to following the exploits on your favorite television show.

Did you know the same social media networking sites you make friends with online can be the same social media networking sites that help your business attract more customers?

It is called social media marketing, and every business operating in every niche needs to have a social media marketing strategy.

What is Social Media Marketing?

Also referred to as the acronym SMM, social media marketing represents a powerful type of digital marketing that encompasses the creation of content that is shared on social media networking websites. The primary goal of social media marketing is to promote your brand to potential customers of your business. Another important goal of SMM is to engage loyal customers by offering a wide variety of new products and services.

Social media marketing should be the promotional cornerstone of any business, but especially businesses that frequently juggle their product and service

It Starts with a Well-Thought Out Plan

Like any online marketing strategy, you need to devise a carefully scripted series of steps to implement a social media marketing campaign successfully. You want to consider a handful of important business goals, before creating a list of questions that you must provide answers.

Here are the handful of questions to ask for developing an effective SMM program:

- Who is part of your target audience?
- How does your target audience use social media networks?
- What message or message do you want your target audience to receive on social media networking websites?
- What do you want your business to achieve by implementing a SMM strategy?

The type of business you own also plays a huge role in devising a well-though out social media marketing plan. For example, a restaurant owner engages customers online by running recipe contests, while the manager of an auto dealership announces short term specials.

Benefits of Social Media Marketing

Think about the return on your time investment by spending no more than five hours a week increasing the exposure of your company online. That is about what it will take for you to reach more customer prospects as well as the loyal patrons of your business, by implementing a well-conceived social media marketing campaign. Around an astounding 90% of Internet marketers responded in a study that social media marketing instantly produced more exposure for their products and services.

Real time exposure equals more customers and hence, an increase in sales.

Let's look at some of the benefits delivered by social media marketing.

A Boost in Search Engine Rankings

By now, you should be aware of the power generated by organic search engine rankings. With organic search engine rankings you do not have to pay for online advertising and in turn, you enjoy an increase in website traffic. Search engine optimization (SEO) is a vital element of any digital marketing strategy. Recent trends demonstrate the big three search engines (Google, Bing, Yahoo) are placing more emphasis on social media sites when calculating search engine rankings. Social Media Examiner released data from a study showing nearly 60% of digital marketers that have used social media marketing techniques for more than a year reported an improvement in search engine rankings for their business websites.

Better Conversion Rates

It is one thing to attract more visitors to your business website. It is quite another thing to convert your website visitors into customers. With an increase in where your business ranks in search engines, you have completed the first step towards converting more website visitors. Social media marketing helps your business present a positive impression by personally interacting with visitors to your social media pages. People prefer to conduct business with people, not faceless companies that present a less than personable image. More than 50% of online marketers stated that by taking the time to develop personal relationships on social media sties, they were able to attract more customers to drive an increase in sales.

Obtain Immediate Customer Feedback

Although Yelp and Google reviews will help you learn more about how customers feel about your brand, you obtain a much better and often times a clearer idea about how your customers feel by engaging them on social media platforms. Not only do you feel the pulse of your customers, social media marketing allows you to respond to dissatisfied customers in real time. Responding to customer feedback in real time represents one of the most effective ways to build customer loyalty.

Cost Effective Way to Attract Customers

No other digital marketing strategy is more cost effective than the many techniques you have available to promote your products and services on social media networking sites. All you have to do is sign up for accounts that typically are free. You can use paid advertising on social media sites to attract customers, but by simply engaging your customers in real time or close to it, you can attract more customers without having to spend money doing it. Moreover, you do not have to spend as much time implementing social media marketing techniques as the time you have to spend on other digital marketing options.

As we know, time equals money.

Proven Social Media Marketing Tips

When asked whether they have or plan to start a social media marketing campaign, most business owners offer the following response: "I don't have the time for it."

Starting a social media marketing program can overwhelm the savviest business owners. However, you don't have to attract millions of followers on Twitter or run a powerful brand marketing campaign on Facebook to reap the benefits of social media marketing.

All you have to do is follow a few time-tested tips.

You Need a Plan

You understand that every successful business strategy starts by developing a well thought out plan. Establishing a social media marketing campaign is not any different than deciding what products to include in an upcoming promotion.

The lack of planning in a social media program will mean the lack of establishing goals. After all, you need to have goals to measure how well your social media program performs.

Here are some elements of a carefully planned social media marketing program:

- Competitor research
- What do you want to accomplish on social media sites?
- Establish evaluation metrics
- Gain inspiration from successful social media marketers

One of the most important phases of the planning process involves creating a calendar that keeps you on track for making significant contributions to your chosen social media networks.

What Social Media Platforms Make the Most Sense?

Making assumptions about which social media platforms makes the most sense for your business but can lead you down a frustrating path. For example, a millennial entrepreneur might assume that Snapchat and Instagram are the two ideal social media platforms to attract like-minded millennials. However, research data demonstrates more than 80% of all millennials still use Facebook to connect with friends, family member, and professional peers. Research the demographic groups that use each of the primary social media platforms. Just as important, stay abreast of recent upstarts that cater to your target audience.

Speaking of Target Audience

Social media marketing for small and medium businesses provides you with the right tools to target your audience. However, you must first define your target audience.

You can acquire gigabytes of data that describes your current customers, as well as use proven social media analytics to discover the members of your target audience. The goal is to produce a comprehensive profile of the typical person that likes to interact with you on social media sites.

Create Lasting Relationships

Social media has the same power of a Smartphone. It allows you to speak directly to followers in real time. Of course, by speaking, we mean writing compelling words that reach the people that are following you on a social media site.

Here's an eye opening statistic for small and medium business owners: More than 90 percent of people that follow small and medium businesses on social media sites plan to make purchases from the same small and medium businesses.

By establishing a presence on social media sites, you have the opportunity to build lasting relationships by interacting with your followers. Lasting relationships mean you will develop a growing number of long time patrons of your business.

Grow Your Audience

After you define your target audience and then begin to attract them to your social media pages, the time has come to develop a strategy that brings more of your target audience on board. For example, if you run a cycling shop in Denver and you have done a good job of attracting avid cycling enthusiasts to your Instagram pages, then you should consider expanding your audience to include cycling fans that live in Boulder, Colorado Springs, and even out of state in cities such as Las Vegas and Phoenix.

You can also implement the best social media marketing practices that attract more customers from your local market. The owner of the Denver cycling shop can upload "How to…" videos on the business YouTube account to reach more potential customers that live in the Mile High City.

Visual Appeal Rules Social Media

The YouTube example is especially relevant because it emphasizes the importance of uploading visually appealing videos, photos and other types of images to your social media pages. Twitter released data taken form an internally conducted study that demonstrated followers of the social media platform are three more times likely to engage with tweets containing a visual element like a photo, video, or image. Another study showed more than 50 percent of millennials make travel plans based on images they saw on social media sites. Snapchat, Pinterest, and Instagram are particularly effective social media sites for uploading images.

Quality Matters, Not Quantity

Yes, the vast number of social media marketing options appears to be much more than the typical small and medium size business owner can handle. After all, you have your plate full running promotions, improving the merchandising plan, and hiring the best employees.

You can overcome the responsibility of implementing a social media marketing campaign by focusing on the quality of your content.

Social media marketing does not mean you have to get up before the crack of dawn each day and upload words of wisdom to one or more social media platforms. In fact, by concentrating on just one or two days a week, you ensure the content you present to your followers offers solutions to common problems.

For example, let's assume you own an auto repair shop. You hop on Facebook one day to see a message left by a follower who plans to rotate the tires on a brand new vehicle. Time is not of the essence, yet you engage the follower by referring them to your Facebook page where you have uploaded a video explaining the step-by-step process of rotating tires on a car.

Twitter is the only social media site that requires you to visit it every day. Otherwise, upload quality content to the other social media platforms in your lineup once, maybe twice a week.

Some Tools are Better than Others

Professional carpenters understand the importance of stocking their tool boxes with tools they plan to use for a project. The same principle should apply to small and medium size businesses that want to monitor the effectiveness of their social media marketing programs.

You need the right tools to succeed.

Here are the four broad categories of tools that help you launch a successful social media marketing campaign:

- Analytics
- Follower engagement management
- Content curation
- Graphics

Analytic tools are the most important tools to have for monitoring the effectiveness of your social media marketing campaign. https://www.brandwatch.com produces extensively detailed reports that allow you to allocate your time and resources to implement the most powerful social media marketing practices. https://www.hootsuite.com is a site that not only gives you an idea about your followers, it also conveniently organizes all of the mentions and messages online that refer to your business.

Best Platforms for Social Media Marketing

You cannot manage every social media account at one time. Now that we have said it, the next question is where should you spend your time engaging your customers on social media sites? The answer depends mostly on where your target audience goes to engage with businesses online. It is not a strictly demographic answer, but demographics do play an important role as to which social media sites your target audience accesses

The primary key to launching and managing a successful social media marketing program is to select the right social media sites to engage your target audience. Go with two, maybe three of the following social media marketing platforms, and you should be able to engage your target audience.

Twitter

If you've heard of a mulligan in golf, then you will understand that Twitter does not count as one of the two, maybe three social media sites your business should be using.

Twitter is a must for every small and medium size business.

The main reason for Twitter's appeal is that the social media giant allows business owners to communicate with customers in real time. With just a couple hundred of characters permitted for each tweet, you can get your message across in a short amount of time.

Real time communication gives you the power to handle customer complaints promptly, as well as inform your followers about an upcoming engagements and specials. Twitter is a powerful tool for service oriented businesses that rely on providing superior customer service to set the standard for quality in their operating niches. With about 330 million active users across the world, Twitter offers advertising opportunities for businesses that want to present targeted promotional messages to the right audience 24 hours per day, seven days a week.

Facebook

Facebook offers small and medium businesses several tools to reach the proper target audience. The leading social media site offers the most diverse membership, with the all-important age group between 24 and 35 years of age representing the largest demographic group. Almost three-quarters of online users that possess incomes greater than $75,000 spend time interacting on Facebook. The company's targeted digital advertising platform optimizes the return on investment for marketing dollars. Facebook is the best social media site for getting your brand's message in front of the right target audience.

Facebook is considered the best social media site for integrating eCommerce platforms. This allows to put your digital store in front of more potential customers. Purchasing a product from your digital store via Facebook requires the click of just one button.

Instagram

With more than 700 million active users, Facebook-owned Instagram has emerged as the premier social media site for uploading images and videos. Once considered the ideal social media platform to share photos and videos with friends and family members, Instagram has become a popular social media platform for brands to gain more exposure among customer prospects. In fact, BrandWatch released a study indicating more than 50% of Instagram users follow brands on the social media network.

If you run a business that has a target audience of consumers under the age of 30, then Instagram is a must have site to include in your social media marketing campaign. By describing your company's unique vision and story through images and videos, you will appeal to a generation that loves to be entertained visually. Instagram offers an easy to use tool that allows you to tell your brand's story, including the popular behind the scenes feature that takes visitors to your Instagram page to the heart of your business.

YouTube

Back in 2006 when Google brought YouTube into the search engine giant's fold, many digital marketing experts said it would be only a matter of time before YouTube pages began to rank high in Google's rankings list.

The experts were right.

YouTube has perhaps the largest age demographic as the foundation of its user network. Running from 18 to nearly 50 years old, your business has a vast base of new customers to attract. YouTube is an especially strong social media site for businesses that upload "How to…" videos. For example, an auto repair shop can present a video describing how to perform a flawless oil change. A bakery can upload video content that explains how to create a wide variety of yummy masterpieces.

YouTube offers businesses the opportunity to create channels that are devoted exclusively to their brands. The social media site also dedicated an unlimited amount of video hosting for companies of all sizes. If you want your business to get noticed online, there is not a more effective way of accomplishing the goal than by starting a YouTube channel for your business.

LinkedIn

Some of your best customers will be professionals that have the disposable income to become repeat patrons of your business. What is the best way to reach professionals online?

You guessed it: LinkedIn.

We are not talking about just the professionals in your business niche. We are talking about reaching out to professionals in every business niche. LinkedIn offers users the opportunity to write articles that help other professionals solve difficult problems. Like Facebook, you can request members of LinkedIn to join your network. The social media site dedicated to professionals gives you a powerful tool to announce upcoming discount programs, as well as recruit suppliers for your products. Instead of attending networking events, you can network with professionals every day by accessing your LinkedIn page. Microsoft owns LinkedIn, which gives the social media site a substantial amount of financial resources to increase the number of user-friendly tools and features.

18

Pricing

Pricing

Remember that whatever you are marketing, it has value to someone or some organization, and they will pay you for it. Marketing is responsible for setting the price that the customer pays. Many times it's the Product Managers, Marketing and Sales executives that work together to set the price.

Good Technical Marketing allows you to avoid competing on price. If you compete on price, you must have the lowest price so you can outlast the war, but this really eats into your margins. Some would argue that good marketing involves a mix of the 4 P's: Price, Product, Place and Promotion. You can't win on price alone, so you need to create messaging that drives the other pieces. Also consider that just about everything is purchased online these days.

The start of every good Technical Marketing campaign is the target – the target market. Always know who your target customer is, in all segments and in all pricing tiers. You have control over your target customers. The external factors you don't have control over, although some larger companies might think they do.

A bullet proof competitive advantage results from a good Technical Marketing program. It allows you to

create a sustainable competitive advantage over time, without having to let competitors influence your price.

Pricing is typically driven and influenced by three things:

- Cost
- Customer
- Competition

You need to cover your costs at a minimum and then you determine what margin you need for profitability. You determine what your customer will be willing to pay and set your price. All of your competitors that haven't read this book, will try to compete on price. You know better by now, and hopefully as a result of reading this book, have developed a strategy that will allow you to compete on everything except price. This gives you freedom to set your price. If you compete on price alone and do not have a good Technical Marketing strategy, you will lose the war.

One of the things that is critical to setting price is answering the question, o what price will convince the buyer to buy? That can be answered by setting your baseline price be determining what is the absolute best price we can offer customers for our products and/or services, then Define Value. Determining value drives up your pricing. And awesome value is obtained from your Technical Marketing program. The better the Technical Marketing program you, the higher the price you can charge. At the end of the day, you need to be able to communicate and articulate that value to the customer.

"

One thing to ultimately keep in mind is that prices are justified by the economics of the customer, not the economics of your cost/profit structure.

"

Retail Pricing

There are essentially two categories in Business-to-Consumer or Retail Goods and Services. There are Products and Services.

Products

There are Products – tangible goods that you can put your hands on and consume. Some of the parameters to consider when pricing Products, brands, and packaging:

- Licensing
- Weight (package or loose)
- Units/Counts/Pieces (single or 12 pack) (Package or Loose)
- Volume (gas, milk) (gallons)
- Weights and Measures
- Subscription or one-off
- Negative Option (Book clubs, don't send me any-more)

Services

There are Services – intangible benefits received as a result of someone performing a service. Some of the parameters to consider when pricing Services.

- Licensing
- Unit price (haircut). Visit
- Length of time. (hourly)
- Yield Management (When/Where/Who) (Time of day, movie, who) (Ticket) (Travel)
- Utilities (water, electricity, garbage, sewer, phones)
- Housekeeping, cleaning, landscaping
- Event (Party)
- Project, Time and Material + profit
- Hourly / with not to exceed cap. (Billing rate)
- Meals (A La carte, fixed, entre, full course)
- % of Media purchase
- Unit pricing for consultants (By the webpage)
- Price per RSS feed, info block
- Rent

Non-Profit Pricing

Non-Profit organizations need to make money too, in order to carry out their mission. A Non-Profit is a legal entity recognized by the government to they basically don't have to pay taxes. Non-Profits still need to make money and can use any of the Business-to-Consumer or Business-to-Business pricing and selling strategies. However, Non-Profits mostly rely on Donations as their revenue stream.

Some of the parameters to consider when pricing Services for Non-Profits:

- Hourly
- Unit
- Class/Semester
- Subscription
- License

Some of the parameters to consider when pricing donations for Non-Profits:

- Amount (Donate $x, you get y)
- Tiered pricing, lumped into categories, $2500, $5000
- Donor level, you get different services at different donor levels
- Sponsorships (tiered also, different levels of recognition)

Government Pricing

The government needs to set prices too. If the Government had a marketing department, or for Government related goods and services, some of the parameters to consider for pricing:

- Taxes (fed,state,property,postage)
- Fees (permits, rent, parcel)
- Use tax. (telecom)
- Licensing/Registration
- Dues
- Membership

Business-to-Business Pricing

In Business-to-Business buyer/seller relationships there is still a customer with economic spending ability and spending patterns. It's just a little different because your products or services are being consumed by another business. Some pricing parameters to consider when selling to a business:

- OEM (sell components that are rebranded, sub-assembly pricing)
- Contractual (Units)
- RFP with contract following
- Licensing
- API's
- Data consumption

Supply Chain Pricing

Supply chain pricing comes into play when you are selling to channel sellers or distribution sellers. Using channels and distribution is an extremely effective way to create economies of scale, in other words, sell more stuff and make alot more money

Some of the parameters to consider when selling into channels and distributers:

- Direct
- Indirect: Retailers/Wholesalers, set your price, so they get their margin
- MSRP (Suggested price)
- Loss leader (base package is free, below their cost) (Advertise a popular product below cost, so you can charge for other items). Marketing sets the price (free), sales sets the discounts/promotions

Product & Service Pricing

One way to determine pricing, is to look at products and services that already exist in the market. Your competitors have done some of the work for you. With old products a market already exists so this is relatively easy to scope. For new products, the market doesn't exist yet, so you have to determine if there are any closely competitive products to draw from. You might have to research how alternative products are priced.

It is true that pricing should cover your costs, but remember it is ultimately determined by how much a customer is willing to pay.

Pricing can also be used competitively to determine different breaking points in the pricing strategy. Ultimately, pricing can be used against your competition to defeat them.

Segmentation Pricing

Segmentation pricing is a method that is used to divide your target market into different segments that require different pricing. Most companies can't afford to offer a one-size-fits-all pricing. It is important to segment the market and price accordingly. Demographics are largely the driver of segmentation pricing based on age, education and perhaps income level. Psychographics can drive your pricing strategy which is based on social value, economic value and impact value. The next time you go to pay for something, look at the product spread offered to you. There is never just one price. There are several prices. Restaurants that are successful know how to keep their menu short and simple, yet offer several options because not every customer will pay the same price. When you go to a car wash, they offer several options – Premium, Gold, Bronze, Silver services ... all based on your spending habits, perceived value and ability to pay.

Variation Pricing

Variation pricing, also sometime called differentiated pricing, refers to the art of creating different categories to fit your target market spending patterns. This is the same as segmentation pricing in that it takes a product or service and creates different levels of pricing to capture the spending habits of your target market. Some examples of variation pricing include:

- Basic/intermediate/pro
- Standard/professional/developer
- Basic/pro/premiere

Discount Pricing

Sometimes you need programs to smooth out the monthly recurring revenue stream. A popular way to do this is offer one-off discount pricing.

Loyalty Pricing

Many business are using Loyalty programs that include discounts, just for loyally spending money with them. A local grocery store here where I live has a grocery loyalty card. I use the card when I shop in the store and when I use it online. After I spend so many dollars on food that I have to buy anyway, I get anywhere from $.10-$.50 cents off at their gasoline pumps. They've got me locked in. I won't but stuff anywhere else unless there is a product they don't carry. Discount cards and Loyalty cards keep the customer coming back.

Types of Buyers

The type of buyer will also determine your price or price spread. Depending on the business, buyers that percieve greater value will generally find more money to spend than people who don't. Some types of buyers to be aware of and their ability to spend:

- Personal vs. Business
- New to Market vs. Experienced Buyers
- Light Users vs. Heavy Users
- Students/Retired vs. Employed
- Peak-Usage vs. Off-Peak Usage

Missionary Pricing

The missionary strategy has been successful in the past with the greatest marketing document ever written – the bible. In the missionary strategy you expand your target market by creating people or business that need your product. For example, sending missionaries to remote nations to help people see the value in the service, only to sell and distribute more bibles, with the ultimate goal of creating loyal followers of God. Another example might be providing free piano lessons, to sell more pianos. Some of these efforts require spending money on these campaigns without any immediate or traceable return. This is called marketing with a "loss leader" because you are leading your marketing and pricing campaign with activities that simply incur a loss.

Bundle Pricing

Bundle pricing works. They get me every-time on Amazon. Bundle pricing works by offering two or more products together but then discounting the entire bundle. For example, on Amazon people who bought that book also bought this one, so if you buy books A+B+C, then you will get 3 for the price of 2. This strategy appeals to buyers who are convinced of your value, and will spend more for additional value because they inherently trust you as the provider of good value. To your business, this is a great way to uplift revenue and move more product at the point of sale.

Current vs. New Customers

One thing to remember is that it is cheaper to keep current customers, than to try and get new customers, or to try to change behaviors of customers loyal to other companies. [quote]

Once you have built your stream of products/services and customer you will need to understand that 20% of customers buy 80% of your product - these are the loyal, heavy users. Make sure you pay close attention to this group. You can increase revenue by offering more to them. Whatever you do, don't lose them or alienate them.

A good example of alienation is sometimes played out for us in the public media when a celebrity contracted with a business to be their "marketing message" gets caught doing something that is perceived to be illegal or unethical. The business immediately drops the celebrity's contract because the business has a loyal target set of customers, and that celebrity just did something to alienate them. The business will have to rebuild its loyalty with those customers all over again – obviously without the celebrity.

Observant Pricing

You might have an idea of what your pricing strategy will be, but you are still unsure. Observant pricing allows you to observe characteristics that signal buyers price sensitivity. You set your prices and observe. To manipulate spending in other categories you offer upgrades or discounts to see if there is a propensity to assimilate buyers into your brand.

Tactic Pricing

Tactic pricing is using some type of tactic to help gauge, set or reset your pricing. These tactics can also be used to determine price sensitivity in either direction, up or down, or bundled. This is similar to Observant pricing. Some examples of pricing tactics are:

- Buyer Identification
- Time of Purchase
- Purchase Location
- Volume or Quantity
- Product Bundling
- Tie-Ins
- Metering

Skim Pricing

Skim pricing is seen typically in goods or services that claim a Premium level of value, but expect fierce competition. This is sometimes seen in the tech industry in a new market segment. The first business to arrive will set its price really high, knowing it will get some buyers, only to enjoy the high margins for a short time until competitors arrive. This works in market segments where there are early adopters and a blue ocean.

This works for some sparse opportunities, but be very cautious, as what you might think is worthy of skim pricing, might not be in the mind of the consumer, and you will price yourself out of the market. If you have any competitors lurking in the shadows they will see this and each your lunch.

Perfect Pricing

So how do you set the perfect price? Good question and the answer is, its more of an art form than a specific formula. But if I had to apply a formula to the art form it would look something like the following.   First determine the highest price someone

Perfect Price

Where:
   H = the highest price someone would pay
   L = the lowest price someone would pay
   V = the value bump
   P = the perfect price someone would pay

Value bump:
$$V = H / L$$

Perfect Price:
$$P = L + V_{[+]}$$

would pay for your product or service (H). Second determine the lowest price someone would pay for your product or service (L). Divide the Highest Price (P) by the Lowest Price (P) and that should give you what I would call the "Value Bump". The Perfect Price (P) then would equal the Lowest Price (L) plus one or more Value Bumps (V). The Value Bump is what you add to the Lowest Price to reflect the value your product or service provides. You may need to add more Value Bumps, depending on the perceived value of your product or service. You have to get something in return for the value your product or service provides and this is the place for that. My only recommendation here is try to keep this simple.

Sweet Spot

So how do you find the Sweet Spot price? Another good question. The way to start out is using the Perfect Pricing estimation model. Then over time, through experimentation in the marketplace, you can fine tune the price. It could even be a combination of pricing practices and experimentation together with your gut feeling.

19

Growth Hacking

As we have seen in previous chapters, digital marketing is replete with memorable catchphrases, some of which have staying power and some of which that disappear as fast as a deleted email. Do you remember when we talked about a product teardown? Well, we have a relatively new marketing term to discuss called growth hacking. Growth Hacking is just another term for Market Hacking™, and it sounds really cool.

Growth hacking refers to a broad term describing several different strategies implemented for achieving growth. Most of the time, the term is applied to early-stage new businesses that need to grow quickly in a short period. The growth must not only be quick, it must also happen by operating on a shoestring business budget.

> **Market Hacking is a combination of methods to increase the speed of getting to market and generating revenue.**

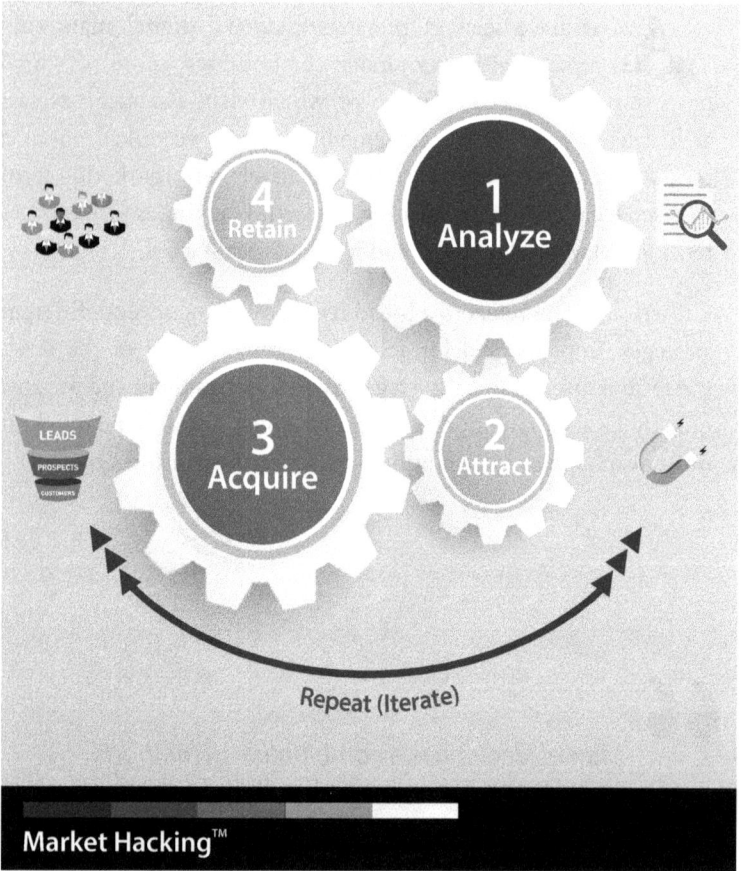

Market Hacking™

215

As the primary goal of implementing a growth hacking strategy, you want to attract as many users or as many customers as possible, without having to spend much money acquiring the users and customers.

Overview of Growth Hacking

Also referred to as market hacking, growth hacking received an increase in attention when some digital marketers linked the term with technical marketing. In fact, you can find technical marketing prints all over growth hacking strategies. Technical marketing should be integrated into growth hacking strategies to optimize your competitive advantage. We want Delta results for technical marketing and when we combine technical marketing with growth hacking, we are looking at a truly explosive marketing combination.

An Automated Sales Process (ASP) represents the primary model that supports growth hacking strategies. It is a fluid loop focusing on how to acquire new customers, retain them, and then utilize the base of new customers to acquire more customers. Think of the gears driving a wheel and you have the mechanical version of growth hacking.

Here are the "gears" that drive growth hacking strategies within the ASP paradigm:

- First impressions
- Engage and educate
- Follow up
- Sales technology
- Referrals and retentions

Instead of rinse and repeat, we retain and repeat.

Profile of a Typical Growth Hacker

In the simplest term, a growth hacker represents a professional who implements creative and inexpensive business strategies to attract and retain new customers. However, growth hackers are not considered just marketers. They also can be product managers and product engineers.

So, what is the profile of the typical growth hacker? Is it someone that has embarked on a mission to start a new business? Well, yes that is the typical profile of a growth hacker. However, we want to focus on three essential traits growth hackers possess.

The typical growth hacker does three things:

- Develop, prioritize, and implement cutting edge growth strategies
- Focuses exclusively on strategies that help their businesses grow
- Tests and analyzes different growth strategies to determine which strategies work well

How Growth Hacking Works

You can call it an integral part of the ASP paradigm or you can call it anything you want, but the Analyze-Attract-Acquire-Retain (AAAR) model is the heart of growth hacking.

Let's look at the four vital components of a growth hacking strategy.

Analyze

This is where technical marketing comes into play. Analyze everything from the identification of your hard-core target audience to the products and services that will allow you to

> *Market Hacking boils down to four words:*
>
> *Analyze ~ Attract ~ Acquire ~ Retain*

grow your business quickly. Make sure you also do the Technical Marketing analysis using the wheel of death and domination.

Attract

Attracting new customers should be mostly about implementing digital marketing programs.

- Search Engine Optimization (SEO)
- Search Engine Marketing (SEM)
- Social Media Marketing (SMM)
- Content Marketing
- Email Marketing
- Video Marketing

YouTube has morphed into a highly effective strategy for attracting potential customers. Since Google purchased the online video platform, the search engine giant has placed more emphasis on getting YouTube pages ranked on the first page of search engine results.

219

Acquire

Acquiring new customers is all about conversions. You analyzed your core target market and implemented strategies to stir interest in your brand. Now comes the hard part. You have to convince customer prospects to trust your startup enough to give it a chance by purchasing a product or a service.

Retain

How does your startup retain customers? The answer is by offering the highest quality products and services that deliver superior value. You can offer discounts for referrals, as well as run contests to reward the loyal customers of your startup.

Remember that each of the four components of a growth hacking strategy are not run independently of each other. Instead, the four growth hacking components usually happen at the same time.

The Important Role of Analytics for Growth Hacking

Each of the four components that comprise the acronym AAAR require well-thought out strategies to make the components work. Of the four parts of AAAR, analytics is the one that presents the most challenges for digital marketers.

Let's review the purpose of analytics for developing a successful growth hacking program.

Analytics Allow Growth Hackers to Change Strategies Quickly

When you have a system in place to tracking and measuring the success of your products, you are able to shift your attracting, acquiring, and retaining strategies quickly. For example, let's assume one of your retention strategies involves rewarding customers that have done business with you over a certain period. A year is a good time frame to use for rewarding loyal customers. After analyzing the spending patterns of your loyal customers, you realize the one-year minimum set for rewarding customer loyalty should be lowered to six months. More customers receive rewards and in return, you measure an uptick in repeat business.

Analytics Confirms Successful Growth Hacking Strategies

Growth hacking analytics not only gives you the tools to make changes to your growth hacking program, it also confirms the success of other growth hacking strategies. A prime example of a growth hacking strategy is a Google AdWords campaign that delivers a positive return on your marketing investment. With the data in place confirming success of the AdWords campaign, you can divert additional resources into the campaign to attract more potential customers. Confirming successful growth hacking strategies ensures you optimize the spending of your digital marketing dollars.

Analytics Gives You a Glimpse into the Future

Entrepreneurs in the midst of getting a startup company up to speed place numerous bets on the future performance of the company. Some of the analytics used to predict the future includes predicting what the competition will do in terms of product rollouts and pricing platforms. Think of this hockey analogy: Growth hacking analytics allows you skate to where the puck travels, instead of going to where the puck used to be. The future of your startup depends somewhat on how well you can predict the future by analyzing business trends.

How to Start a Growth Hacking Program

You are now highly motivated to make growth hacking work for you. The question now is how to get started towards the ultimate goal of attracting, acquiring, and retaining more customers. The first step should be to introduce a product that you can analyze at different price points. You will gather important data that will drive future business decisions. In addition, you will understand what the buyer personas are for each of the products tested.

The next step involves using analytical data at specified intervals to update different elements of a product. Customer feedback is also an important part of starting a successful growth hacking program. Market each of the products tested to attract and acquire more customers. A/B tests and other types over customer conversion tactics are an important component for starting a successful growth hacking program.

Growth Hacking Strategies that Work

What growth hacking strategies have a proven record of success? The answer are most of the usual digital marketing suspects.

- Develop an SEO-friendly website
- Running a blog
- Guest blogging
- Uploading regularly scheduled podcasts
- Hosting webinars
- Offering free eBooks that help customer prospects solve problems
- Have a huge social media presence
- Send in opt-in email newsletters
- Implement the latest Google-approved SEO strategies

Examples of Growth Hacking Success

What startups have morphed into powerful online businesses because of the successful implementation of growth hacking programs? Dropbox rewards loyal users of the file hosting service for recruiting new users. The reward historically has been the addition of storage for organizing files. Outlook appends a line for each email sent out to ask regular users of the service to sign up new users. Airbnb leverages Craigslist to promote affordable accommodations to new users of the online marketplace and hospitality service.

What is the Growth Hacking Sales Funnel?

You have at least heard about sales funnels, if not put the proven digital marketing practice to good use for your business. Many digital marketers compare sales funnels to the funnel we use to pour oil into a car's engine. With a wide opening at the top, the oil moves down a funnel that becomes smaller until the oil reaches its intended target.

Does the same principle work for a growth hacking sales funnel?

If you plan to introduce a new product, the primary goal of a growth hacking funnel is to attract new customers. This is often achieved by motivating customer prospects to visit your website or an app that you design specifically for the product's introduction. Since most customer prospects are simply visitors to the app or the startup website, you want to "funnel" them into a relationship that results in more sales.

Visits are not Enough

You are not a true growth hacker, if you believe visits to your app or website are enough to convert potential customers. The goal changes from attracting customer prospects to turning them into active new customers. Also referred to as customer activation, the process of customer conversions via the growth hacking funnel establishes a long lasting relationship between you the entrepreneur and the customers that define your target audience. Activation happens when potential customers of your startup join an email list, start an account on the company website, subscribe to a service or even make a product purchase online or in person.

The Customer Relationship is Based on Trust

You have funneled numerous customer prospects to your business. Some of the new customers have even purchased a few of your products. The final part of a growth hacking sales funnel is for your new customers to transition into long time patrons of your business. How do you accomplish the transition to lifelong loyal customers?

You build customer relationships based on trust.

Building trust with your new customers begins by your startup establishing credibility, which you create by offering superior products. After new customers see how well a product works, they are more likely to trust your business and purchase other products offered by your company.

The growth hacking funnel works in many ways like the classic sales funnel. However, the main difference between the two funnels is past performance matters more for growth hacking funnels.

If you have read this entire chapter, then you are interested in applying growth hacking strategies to grow your startup. Like other types of marketing strategies, growth hacking, or market hacking represents a set of skills you have to learn, and that is the second difference between sales funnels and growth hacking funnels. Most sales funnels require a few innate skills that cannot be taught. For growth hacking, you can learn how to attract, acquire, and retain customers. Moreover, you can learn the skills needed to analyze data and boost the performance of your startup.

Growth hacking is not a one and done deal. You will make mistakes and by learning from the mistakes, you should be able to hone your growth hacking strategies to improve the performance of your startup.

20

The VC

The VC

A lso known as the "Money Mafia", Venture Capitalists (VC) are an important function in the any business setting. You don't have to know them personally, although it might help, you just have to know how that system works. We are all in this business together, so don't feel like you have to be left out of this secret knowledge.

Silicon Valley was once considered the innovation engine of the world, and also the evaluation engine of the world. Although some would like you to believe that New York City is such a place along with Washington DC. It is true that investors flock to NYC and there is a modicum of power in DC, however, the birthplace and residence of innovation power has historically been established in the Silicon Valley. If you want to do business, you had to have a presence in the Silicon Valley, it just worked that way.

However, with the rising cost of living in California, many people are leaving. The next hotspot of innovation and investment will likely be in other cities such as Denver, and smaller hubs where there is a thick talent pool and a reasonable cost of living.

Whether you are working for a large company, or starting out in your garage like the Packard fella's did, you need to understand the money engine, because you will eventually need to know how to put this engine to work. As investors will tell you, today is always a great time to start a company. Some brilliant companies get financed and funded in economic downturns. Most companies that "can" raise money, do, even when it is hard to raise money in economic downturns. In fact, the best time to find deals is in a downturn. Remember Warren Buffets comment that "Pessimism is your friend, optimism is your enemy".

When large companies face a difficult future, there is huge opportunity for new ones. Whether the economy is up or down, it is good to look at the VC "resource pool". Your resources are the investors as well as the talent pool that exists, those people that are available to hire. A downturn is the best time to start milking the hiring pool, some of the best talent may have been discarded erroneously by a larger company. In large companies, the top decision makers rarely have visibility of the talent at lower levels and eventually discard people without knowing the valuable organ they have just lopped off. One mans trash is another mans treasure.

There are "Pools of Money" characterized by the stage of the venture capital funding behavior they engage in. There are Angel investors, Private investors, Crossover investors and Public investors.

Angel's invest small amounts to get companies "off the ground" or bootstrapped. Angel investors only invest in things that will be potentially big. Going from Angel to profitability is highly dependent on the investor eco-system. Angel's try to get out at 5x return on their money. Angel investors will play depending on how much money they have in their budget.

Private investors are a source for larger funds, the Series A, B, C round's of financing.

Crossover ventures help in taking privately invested companies "over" to the public market, hence crossover.

Public investors buy and sell on money markets, commonly associated with Wall Street. This is where the Initial Public Offering (IPO) makes its debut.

Each of these investors makes up the "Pool of Money", and they need to be active to fuel the entrepreneurial funding engine. Each of these investors needs to know there will be a buyer in the next market.

There is a sequence of investing events that need to happen. Angel investors sell to Private investors. Private investors sell to Crossover ventures. Crossover ventures sell to the Public.

Angels will fund anywhere from 3-4 companies a year. Private investors will fund anywhere from 10-20 companies a year. Crossover ventures will fund anywhere from 6-10 companies a year.

There are typically 3 stages to a startup company. Early stage, Crossover stage, and Public stage.

Angels and Private investors play in the Early stage. Crossover's bridge the gap between private and public stages. The public stage is where the company has established itself and seeks to be acquired, hence the exit strategy. There is always an exit strategy.

If there is no IPO market, then Mergers and Acquisitions (M&A) may be the next option.

A less fortunate by-product is the concept of an Incubator, where someone invests a sum of money in the hopes that something good will come out of the oven. Because there isn't much thought and planning involved, Incubators don't really amount to much, because there is no direction or successful business plan. They eventually fall by the wayside, because they don't produce value – a direct result of a failed business plan.

Special Private Acquisition Companies (SPACs) have gone by the wayside. These are companies that raise public capital and then buy small companies in the hopes they will bring a return. A nice idea but these don't perform well, and in a downturn, they disappear.

The Inside Round is an "on the table" round, or a deal made on a table informally with an investor. It is not strange to see these done on a napkin at a restaurant. The pools of money will do one of these a year, but really need to seek additional private investment to get the company to profitability.

VC's often refer to what they like to call a "Liquidity Event". Investors like to see liquidity, or cash, so they can go out and make other investments. When they are determining whether or not to invest, in the back of their minds they are always trying to determine when this Liquidity Event or next buyer in the pool will come along. Will they get a return on their money in 12 months or 3 years? Typically, the VC need to see

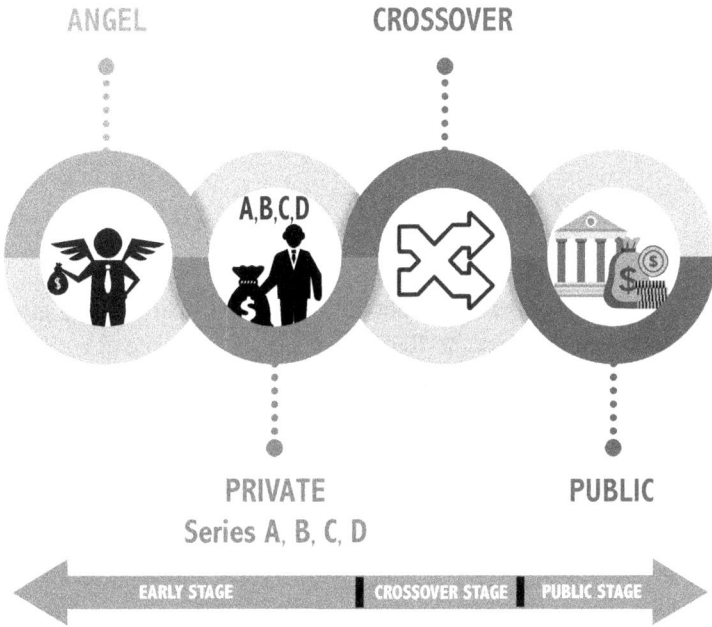

ANGEL CROSSOVER

A,B,C,D

PRIVATE PUBLIC
Series A, B, C, D

EARLY STAGE | CROSSOVER STAGE | PUBLIC STAGE

a liquidity event within 3 years. Otherwise, they might be err'ing on the thought that this venture will not be fruitfull.

Angels, or early stage investors, rarely think in terms of revenue multipliers. The "Revenue Multiple" is more prevalent in the private investor arena, and used to determine what the fair investment price is that will lead to the next round of investment.

A trend that has evolved through whatever means, called the 90/20 rule. As it turns out there are the "Top 20" venture firms that deliver 90% of the returns in the venture capital arena. Outside of that, it is a funding "no-mans land". Some of these firms are just machines and know what they are doing. Others are trying to figure out what they are doing. Either way, this shouldn't deter you from venturing in.

What the VC's look for

When you go to the pool of money to borrow, make sure you have a plan. Remember earlier we talked about just getting started, how you don't really need a 200 page business plan? This is where you need the long, thorough business plan. It doesn't need to be 200 pages, but it does need to be longer that 20. You can almost view these guys as loan underwriters looking at your "loan package". Before they lend on you, some key components must exist to make them feel like you are a safe bet. Because, in reality, only 1 out of 10 deals is going to be successful in the investor's portfolio.

Make sure you have a solid plan. Your business plan must show how you intend to get to profitability. The product must be viable. Demonstrate who your customers are, who will buy, and how it feeds your revenue engine. Some of the things that should be considered, and that will make your proposal more desirable, are stability aspects that show you have skin in the game. The old fashioned way of starting a company is not to take salaries until you get traction. Build credibility first, get some customers under your belt and show a revenue stream. When you do raise money, make sure you raise enough money with enough cushion in the bank to get you to the next stage of investment. Articulate your burn rate. High burn rate companies are harder to get started – because they spend faster than they accumulate.

Does your business model work, and will it take you to the next funding event. What is your "Inter-Fund" strategy. After the internet bubble runoff there were timelines to profitability. Angel investors expect a 7 year timeline to profitability. Angel investors never get the company to profitability, they always seek the next buyer before that happens. Angels try to get the company to the private stage, or Series A investors. The private investors look to take the company to the profitability stage. Private investors typically seek a 5-7 year timeline to profitability. After the Private stage, appropriate valuation kicks in. Appropriate valuation is used to determine how much the company is worth to the next investor.

Build into the plan the following important features.

- How can you make sure the technology works, before you ramp up to spend money?
- How much traction do you have, before you try to borrow money?
- How will you articulate a current, present and active business model?
- How steep, far or long is the revenue "Hockey Stick"?

Despite the process involved to get a company started, the cost of starting a company is much lower than it was 5 to 10 years ago. The internet is one of the few places where you can get a company started, and easily get something going with $100-$500k investment.

Every company in the world is in a state of constant change. Depending on the economic climate globally, it may take a company shorter or longer to get to profitability. The public market must exists, IPO or merger, otherwise the funding engine will dry up and the innovation engine will die. Innovation drives the global economy. In order to be doing IPO's and mergers, there needs to be stability in the public market, otherwise early stage capitalists don't see how they will find a buyer in the next stage of funding.

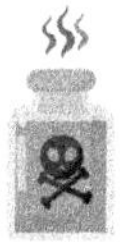

21
Exit Strategy

There is always an exit strategy. Typically, it is either Initial Public Offering (IPO), Merger or Takeover, Sales with valuation or the less desired Fire Sale. Initial Public Offerings generate a lot of cash for the organization and have historically made founders rich. But the revenue in the company and the market has to be there to support the stock price and continued growth. Otherwise, IPO's end up where they started, just a windfall, the founder's cash out and the technology fades. Takeovers still generate cash for the founders and have a higher hope of the technology surviving and taking on new life, and because it is less dependent on capital markets. This has been the exit strategy as of late.

You see the Organization Profile questions being tossed across the table at board meetings and during analyst reviews, but it doesn't hurt to know this language yourself. Because in a few quick sentence's takeover artists, mergers and acquisitions kings can size you up faster than you can blink just by asking some of these key questions. All of which give credence to the performance of an organization or lack thereof, competitively.

Whether this information is used in competitive analysis or not is up to individual preference, and it sometimes is. You most often find this trudgery being dished out to industry analysts so that they can accurately spin your company to the street or industry.

The answers to the questions on the Organization Profile sheet will allow you to quickly determine how your organization compares to a competitors. Based on these results you can tailor your competitive strategy. Do you have high ground in the marketplace, are you always getting to the customer first, are you winning most of the battles? Is there significant growth in the market to take advantage of or is it time for an acquisition or to be acquired?

22
Illustrious Final Comments

For Professionals

If you are already working in technical marketing, hone your skills. If you are thinking of getting into technical marketing, be it known unto you that you must really enjoy hard work, and must have a natural passion for this type of work. Technical Marketeers love sitting in the lab and plugging in equipment. They love running tests and gathering results. They love looking through test results and competitive data to find a story or a competitive delta that didn't exist before. They love doing research. Some technical marketers take it to the next level and engage in pure strategy and charting strategic direction for the companies they work for. Some technical marketeers find a healthy career in product management and/or product marketing. There are many levels of technical marketing to engage your skills and there is always a lot of work to be done, so find your passion and help create value in bridging the gap between engineering and sales.

For Students

I couldn't decide what to do with my life when I entered college, but I did have what I would call an idea. I entered my first year of college as a Computer Science major. The program got really intense during my Junior year, and I didn't like it. Book learning wasn't for me. We were getting too deep into bits, bytes, gates, ands, nands, ors, microprocessors and such. There were long hours in the labs, writing programs in Pascal to model databases and queueing theory. We built operating systems in assembler language using punch cards on old IBM typewriter machines that were pre-mainframe era. To run the program, you had to stack and feed your cards into the card reader. We carried our programs around in shoeboxes full of punch cards. What was bitterly comical is when the box tipped over and the cards flew out, having to put them back in order by hand manually. In an advanced class I remember using a monochrome (black and white) monitor that ran at 300 baud back to the campus mainframe and I thought this was smokin because it was better than punch cards. The hardest class was #151 and I felt like I needed a bottle of it just to get through. I contemplated hard at changing my major to finance, and even shopped around for different colleges in different parts of the state. I was about to do it, when an HR manager at the company where I was working my summer job told me not to. I will say he was very direct, honest and correct. His experience and wisdom was priceless and very accurate. Nevertheless, he said, "use the talent that you have, get your BS in Computer Science, then get your Masters and you can write your ticket anywhere". Direct or not, he was right. I would have been a terrible lawyer, even though I can read and understand legal briefs and I file my own patents, copyrights and trademarks today. I would have been a terrible doctor, at least I would not have enjoyed it that much. I'm not much of a bean counter. I actually ended up doing what I do best, and I love what I do. All I can say, and it was said to me once. "Do what you like, and like what you do. The rest will fall into place".

245

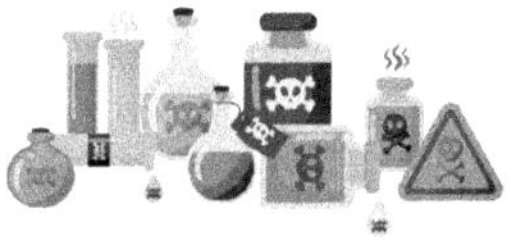

Index

Craig Thomas Ellrod holds a Bachelor of Science in Computer Science from California State University, Chico, and a Master of Business Administration from Pepperdine University. He has been working in the computer industry for over thirty years, and has been working in Cybersecurity since 2005. He has held many positions in the computer industry including software programmer, technical support, field and corporate system engineering, solution architect, technical and product marketing, product management and sales. He has worked for companies such as Celerity Computing, Emulex, Pinnacle Storage, Sync Research, Cisco Systems, Extreme Networks, Citrix Systems, Akamai, Trustwave and smaller startup ventures. He has authored patent applications, patent designs and received an innovation award while at Extreme Networks. Craig is a published author, having written technical books for Packt Publishing. Craig loves to tinker on the Internet having built several blog sites and web sites including, www.sendmykid.com, www.brainiac.academy, www.goodcreds.com, www.craigslaw.org.

Technical Marketing® II

second edition

by
Craig Thomas Ellrod

Technical Marketing
~and~
Technical Marketing II

ISBN 978-0-9822570-4-3

90000

9 780982 257043

trate
uest™

Permissions

Excerpts from "*The Art Of War*", by "*Sun Tzu*", © 1991. Reprinted by arrangement with Shambhala Publications Inc., Boulder, CO. https://www.shambhala.com.

Mention of "*The Art Of Peace*", by "*Morihei Ueshiba*", © 1992, by arrangement with Shambhala Publications Inc., Boulder, CO. https://www.shambhala.com.

Excerpts from "*Marketing Warfare*", by "*Al Ries, Jack Trout*", © 1986, by permission of McGraw-Hill Companies, New York, NY. https://www.mheducation.com.

Mention of "*Blue Ocean Strategy*", by "*W. Chan Kim and Reneé Mauborgne*", © 2005, by permission of Harvard Business School Press, Boston, MA. "*Blue Ocean Strategy*" available at https://www.harvardbusiness.org.

www.ingramcontent.com/pod-product-compliance
Lightning Source LLC
Chambersburg PA
CBHW071337210326
41597CB00015B/1480